Known
&
Loved

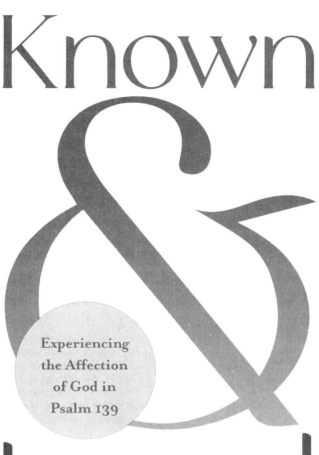

Known

&

Experiencing the Affection of God in Psalm 139

Loved

glenna marshall

MOODY PUBLISHERS

CHICAGO

Edited by Pamela Joy Pugh
Interior design: Brandi Davis
Cover design: Kaylee Lockenour Dunn
Cover element of starlight effect courtesy of Sunset Lovers on Unsplash.

ISBN 978-0-8024-3651-1

Originally delivered by fleets of horse-drawn wagons, the affordable paperbacks from D. L. Moody's publishing house resourced the church and served everyday people. Now, after more than 125 years of publishing and ministry, Moody Publishers' mission remains the same—even if our delivery systems have changed a bit. For more information on other books (and resources) created from a biblical perspective, go to www.moodypublishers.com or write to:

Moody Publishers
820 N. LaSalle Boulevard
Chicago, IL 60610

1 3 5 7 9 10 8 6 4 2

Printed in the United States of America

To the people of Grace Bible Fellowship in Sikeston, Missouri,
with whom I am privileged to worship, serve, and grow in Christ.

You are greatly loved.

Contents

"To be loved but not known is comforting but superficial. To be known and not loved is our greatest fear. But to be fully known and truly loved is, well, a lot like being loved by God. It is what we need more than anything. It liberates us from pretense, humbles us out of our self-righteousness, and fortifies us for any difficulty life can throw at us."

DR. TIMOTHY KELLER[1]

1. Timothy Keller, *The Meaning of Marriage* (Penguin Books, 2011), 101.

Who Is This Book Really About?

I used to think that love was something God doled out with miserly resistance. I pictured Jack Arnold, the disgruntled dad of the 1988 television series *The Wonder Years*, slowly opening his wallet, which creaked with stinginess as he forked out a couple of dollars for Kevin's allowance. Kevin held his breath, eyes fixed on his dad's tight-lipped grimace. A raise in allowance hinged on his ability to either please his father or catch him in a good mood. If his dad was in a bad mood, that wallet would snap shut faster than you could say "please."

How did I come to own this picture of God's love? Too many 1980s sitcoms, perhaps, but mostly, my false view of God's character grew from my own biblical illiteracy. Even after coming to faith in Christ, when I was down or discouraged or when life didn't go as I had hoped, I translated my disappointments as evidence of God's disapproval. In my skewed, experience-based theology, His love was something I had to earn and keep, even after He saved me. *Be good or He'll love you less*—as though God's love were a currency exchanged for one's performance, something that can be lost with bad moods or unchecked boxes on my life's list of good deeds.

Whenever I inventoried my life and the goings-on of my heart with this stingy view of the Almighty, I worried that the thing that kept God from loving me with affection is the fact that He knows me. Really *knows* me. People are quick to say, "God knows your heart!" And I think to myself with doom—*yes, He most certainly does.* I've worried I'll never be able to convince Him He made a good decision in saving me. Though I believed Jesus died to pay for my sins, I wondered if God wanted me to feel unhappy about what it cost—because that's how *He* felt. Unhappy. Regretful. Annoyed.

In recent years, the Lord has unraveled that misunderstanding, restitching together my view of Him with threads of love and faithfulness knotted together so tightly, I doubt I could ever pick them apart. (I pray I never try.) How do you relearn who God is after chasing the coattails of a god you've made in your own image? How do you move from the cranky, disgruntled god whose love is won and lost over and over to the Father whose love is everlasting? How do you stop trying to earn what God made free?

You start with Scripture. You start with God's very words to us about who He is and how He loves us.

A PSALM FOR THE FEARFULLY KNOWN AND QUESTIONABLY LOVED

In the middle of the Bible, near the end of Psalms, we find the answers to our questions about God's love for us. Truthfully, the *entirety* of God's Word is a declaration of underserved love, and we'll explore plenty of it in the pages ahead, but as I've wrestled with my poor understanding of God's opinion of me, it's this one chapter in the middle of my Bible that has helped me unravel my disorderly perceptions and stitch them back together with a biblical thread.

Psalm 139 is a celebration of being known, really *known*—and loved anyway—by God. With verses that lift our chins to look at our Creator, Psalm 139 peels back the layers of who we are as humans upon whom God has set His affections with purpose and loyalty. Nothing is exposed that God doesn't already know about. Though we hide our worst selves so we can be loved according to the world's definition of the word, God knows every dark corner, every awkward angle, every shadowed space. He committed to save and love us anyway. He didn't gradually come to know and love us, and what a relief! His love isn't based on our good traits. He loves us because He loves us. Because He always planned to know us up close and intimately, to set His affections on us as His children. And it is His character to keep His promise to love and save. Not with stinginess or reluctance but with *delight*.

How can the holy, perfect God of the universe stoop so low? How can He love us when He sees the worst in us? When we prop up our sinfulness against His holiness, how can we believe that He loves us?

In the pages ahead, we will answer those questions by walking through Psalm 139, section by section. We'll explore the ways God has ordained and ordered our days. We'll look at what it means to be hemmed in by His presence and why that's not a fearful thing. We'll explore how to live with bodies and minds He carefully knitted together which have unraveled with pain and disorder. We'll examine the ways God's personal love for us can free us from the fear of being alone, forgotten, and ashamed. We'll learn what it means to be truly known and truly loved by the God who sent His Son to pay for our sins at the cross. And we'll learn to celebrate His unfailing love by living in it.

IT'S ALWAYS ABOUT HIM

This book is about you and me and the ways we try to hide what we think makes us unlovable. It's about our desire to be known and yet still somehow loved. But mostly? This book is about God. The Know*er*. The One who loves anyway. It's about the God who decided to love you before He said, "Let there be light." It's about the God who isn't disgruntled or begrudging in His care for you but who is lavish in His affections. It's about the God who isn't cornered by His promise to love us but who is *happy* to keep it, who finds great joy in keeping His promises. It's about the God who knows you better than you know yourself and who loves you wholly, completely, faithfully anyway.

Psalm 139 proclaims what it means to be fully known by God but in a way that brings comfort, joy, and peace rather than shame, doubt, and fear. When we believe that God's opinion of us is not unfavorable, when we get a glimpse of His intentional care for us, when we stop imbuing the God who *is* love with our poor definitions of it—then we will love Him more, for we will better understand that His thoughts toward us are not what we deserve.

Be confident that you have all of God's love in Christ, that you'll never lose it.

As Christians, we often talk about the cross as the epoch or the pinnacle of God's love, confusing His *ultimate* expression of love for His *final* expression of love. But God's love didn't stop at the cross. His love didn't stop when He shone the light of Christ in your heart and gave you saving faith. His love didn't stop once He moved you from death to life, from old creature to new creation. His love didn't stop when He adopted you into His family. No. These were simply your first awakenings to His love for you. He's loving you as generously and lavishly now as He did when He sent Jesus to stand in your place at the cross. He didn't save you in love and then scowl in displeasure when you didn't deserve it. His love continues, no matter how poorly we grasp it. He loves to love you. That's a weird sentence to write and an even weirder one to believe. He loves to love us.

Tim Keller said we grasp God's love for us by meditating on the work of Jesus.[1] When we spend time considering His love, thinking on it, and working it around in our minds, then we become convinced of its truth, depth, and potency.

That is the invitation of this book. To consider His love. To think deeply about His knowledge. To feel secure in its strength. I want you to be confident that you have all of God's love in Christ, that you'll never lose it, that you will never stand before a disgruntled father who is unaccustomed to opening his stores and sharing what he has. That's not the God of the Bible. He is not Jack Arnold who needs a cocktail at the end of a long day of work and whose wallet groans with unaccustomed generosity. God is the Father who runs after the wayward child, who searches high and low for the lost sheep. He doesn't change once the child is home or the sheep is found. He loves. He loves. He *loves.*

Our God is no miserly dad with a creaky wallet. He is a gracious Father whose love predates time itself, was displayed in Christ, and never ends for those who belong to Him. He had to send Jesus because we are so sinful, but He wanted to send Jesus because we are valuable to Him.[2]

God knows you. Inside and out. And He loves you. Inside and out. So let's learn what it means to be *known* so we'll know how to live *loved.*

---

1. Timothy Keller, *Prayer: Experiencing Awe and Intimacy with God* (Penguin Books, 2014), 173.
2. This phrase came from Dr. Timothy Keller, in his sermon, "Running From God," on Jonah 1:1–10 preached at Redeemer Presbyterian Church on September 9, 2001.

O Lord, you have searched me and known me!
You know when I sit down and when I rise up;
you discern my thoughts from afar.
You search out my path and my lying down
and are acquainted with all my ways.
Even before a word is on my tongue,
behold, O Lord, you know it altogether.
You hem me in, behind and before,
and lay your hand upon me.
Such knowledge is too wonderful for me;
it is high; I cannot attain it.

Where shall I go from your Spirit?
Or where shall I flee from your presence?
If I ascend to heaven, you are there!
If I make my bed in Sheol, you are there!
If I take the wings of the morning
and dwell in the uttermost parts of the sea,
even there your hand shall lead me,
and your right hand shall hold me.
If I say, "Surely the darkness shall cover me,
and the light about me be night,"
even the darkness is not dark to you;
the night is bright as the day,
for darkness is as light with you.

For you formed my inward parts;
you knitted me together in my mother's womb.
I praise you, for I am fearfully and wonderfully made.
Wonderful are your works;
my soul knows it very well.

My frame was not hidden from you,
when I was being made in secret,
    intricately woven in the depths of the earth.
Your eyes saw my unformed substance;
in your book were written, every one of them,
    the days that were formed for me,
        when as yet there was none of them.

How precious to me are your thoughts, O God!
    How vast is the sum of them!
If I would count them, they are more than the sand.
    I awake, and I am still with you.

Oh that you would slay the wicked, O God!
    O men of blood, depart from me!
They speak against you with malicious intent;
    your enemies take your name in vain.
Do I not hate those who hate you, O LORD?
    And do I not loathe those who rise up against you?
I hate them with complete hatred;
    I count them my enemies.

Search me, O God, and know my heart!
    Try me and know my thoughts!
And see if there be any grievous way in me,
    and lead me in the way everlasting!

**PSALM
139**

"O LORD, you have searched me and known me!
You know when I sit down and when I rise up;
    you discern my thoughts from afar.
You search out my path and my lying down
    and are acquainted with all my ways.
Even before a word is on my tongue,
    behold, O LORD, you know it altogether."
You hem me in, behind and before,
    and lay your hand upon me.
Such knowledge is too wonderful for me;
    it is high; I cannot attain it.

1

Known to the Core

Does God Even Like Me?

When I was newly married, I started a blog. Back in 2003, blogs were still relatively novel. I found a hosting site that housed forums of blogs so you could share your work with other bloggers writing in your niche. This was before social media became what it is today, so the forums served as a mashup of blogging and networking all in one.

I loved blogging. It gave me a way to use the creative writing skills I'd honed in college, and it provided space to write for an audience. *An audience who had no idea who I was.* This was both the beauty and the oddity of blogging in the early 2000s. Like many other hobby bloggers, I wrote anonymously because I didn't want anyone I knew to find my blog and read it. And yet, I was perfectly fine baring my soul to complete strangers. I wanted to be known, but not *known*. This was controlled transparency. Writing had much less risk when there was no face or name attached to it. I could write with complete honesty about my personal life—but without any negative effects on my personal life. I could hide the parts of my personality or character that were off-putting, so, much like the way social media works today, people didn't know me for who I truly was.

I wanted to be known. I wanted to be loved. But I feared that the one would cancel out the other.

No one on this earth, not even my husband of more than twenty-one years, knows me to the core of who I am. Not even *I* know myself that well, and I like to think I've got a pretty good handle on self-awareness! Have you ever said or done something and then immediately (with great regret) thought, "*Why* did I say that? *What* was I thinking?" Yeah, me too. We often speak or act or make decisions without understanding what led us to do so, unsure of whether that action or decision is consistent with who we think we are. It's not a strange quality to long to be known, to have good working knowledge of self, to understand who we are and why we operate the way we do. But, in our finite limitations, we just can't know everything, not even about ourselves. Omniscience is not a human quality. It's a divine one.

THE GOD WHO KNOWS YOU

When I was a small child, I read a book that explained how you could pray to God anytime and anywhere. The pages were filled with colorful illustrations of people praying in all kinds of scenarios: in traffic, at school, before bed. There was even a picture of a little boy sitting in his tree house while talking to God. Those images have stayed with me for nearly forty years because reading that book was the first time I grasped that God sees and knows everything. I was surprised to learn I didn't have to pray aloud because God hears everything, even the words in my mind and heart. But the Bible takes that concept a step further than the children's book did.

The psalmist writes, "Great is our Lord, and abundant in power; his understanding is beyond measure" (Ps. 147:5). There is no limit to God's knowledge. It isn't just that God hears our internal thoughts and words, it's that He *already* knows them all. God knows our thoughts before we think them, our words before we speak them, our steps before we take them.

Psalm 139:1 sets the stage for the entire passage, declaring to the Lord what we know about His knowledge. "O LORD, you have searched me and known me!" This word *known* isn't referencing a mere acquisition of facts. It's a thorough examination, an intimate evaluation. God has seen every hidden corner of our hearts and every secret thought in our minds. He knows what's in our hearts—truly in our hearts—better than we do.

God is fully familiar with every mundane moment of our ordinary days.

Notice the tense here: *have searched* and *known*. God isn't getting to know you now. He already knows you. It's past tense. (Long past tense. Like, before the universe existed past tense!) He knows who you were, who you are now, and who you will be. He hasn't missed anything. His knowledge of you was thorough and complete before you ever took a breath, before you were even conceived, as we'll discuss in chapter 5.

King David, our psalmist, continues in verses 2–3: "You know when I sit down and when I rise up; you discern my thoughts from afar. You search out my path and my lying down and are acquainted with all my ways." Here, present tense is used. God knows about our current physical activities. He knows when we're lying down to rest or when we get up to work. He is fully familiar with every mundane moment of our ordinary days. He knows that the spot on my lower back aches while I sit on this hard dining room chair to type these sentences. He is aware of how many times I've paused in writing to refill my coffee, check Instagram, respond to the ongoing text thread with my mom and sister.

God's knowledge is limitless, and nothing escapes His notice. He knows about that Cadbury Creme egg I stole from the grocery store when I was five, how I feared death when I was six, how I wanted to follow Jesus when I was seven, how I began to love the Bible when I was twelve, how I wanted to go to the mission field when I was sixteen. He knows that I used to doubt my salvation daily until I understood the efficacy of Jesus' blood when I studied Colossians 2. He knows about the things I've left out of my journal for fear that someone else might read and judge. He knows me on a cellular level, understanding things about my physical body I will never comprehend. He knows about the overactive T cells that attack my spine and joints with inflammatory arthritis. What's more, He knows what each T cell looks like and how it functions. He knows how wrinkled I'll be when I'm eighty, whether I'll even live to be eighty, and the precise moment when I'll close my eyes to this world and open them to His face.

When I was eight or nine years old, I was in the car with my family, and we had stopped at a red light in the middle of town. While we waited for the light to change, I watched a woman in the car next to us. I noticed her haircut and the clothing she was wearing. I wondered where she was going and what her life was like. And then, I felt completely overwhelmed by the fact that she was a whole person with a history and a future and dreams and hopes and a life as wonderfully detailed as mine. There's a name for this sudden realization and intense awakening of your perception of others. It's called *sonder*. The dictionary defines *sonder* as "the feeling one has on realizing that every other individual one sees has a life as full and real as one's own, in which they are the central character and others, including oneself, have secondary or insignificant roles."[3] I often feel sonder when I am sitting in an airport or in a large crowd at a concert or conference. All these people. All these intricate details. God doesn't just know me; He knows us all.

From our curious idiosyncrasies to the outlandish thoughts that keep us awake at night— He is acquainted with all our ways.

So, take all of that intimate past, present, and future knowledge that God has about me and you—and multiply it by billions. Trillions. I have no idea how many people have lived or will live throughout history, but He does. And He knows everything about them. From their life's goals to the number of freckles on their skin—He has known them. From our curious idiosyncrasies to the outlandish thoughts that keep us awake at night—He is acquainted with *all our ways*. All of us. Every human who's ever lived or will live. That's . . . hard to grasp. (Insert a theological feeling of sonder here.)

God knows everything for He created everything. And He called His creation good. His creation of humans He called *very* good. But we know what happened in Eden in Genesis 3. We know that sin entered the world and that everything thereafter was tainted by it. We know that the good things God created bear the curse of sin and death. And here is where our thoughts about God's thoughts go south. We wonder if the fall means that God's knowledge of us is profoundly and *only* negative. When

---

3. Dictionary.com, s.v. "sonder," https://www.dictionary.com/browse/sonder.

we take a good hard look at ourselves, we see our sinfulness and fear God thinks the worst, even in our redeemed, new-creation-in-Christ state. We don't want to accuse God of delighting in someone who sins, so we recast Him as a disapproving Father who is perpetually put out with us. What a disappointment we must be to Him! If He knows us, really knows us like this, shouldn't we be scared?

DOES GOD LIKE ME?

Psalm 139 helps us see how God's intimate knowledge of us should bring us comfort. That, in essence, is the goal of this book: to understand the blessing of being known and loved by God so that we can live confidently in His knowledge and love. We might have no trouble believing that God generally loves His people, but when we consider just how well He knows us, we struggle to believe that God loves us individually. *Me*, individually. *You*, individually. Does He even *like* us?

Maybe you've had questions like these before:

Is God's love personal?
Did He just *barely* allow me into the kingdom?
Is God perpetually disgruntled toward me?
Is He begrudging in His affection?
Did I escape judgment by the skin of my teeth?
Does God keep me at arm's length to remind me of my wretchedness?
Does He stay mad at me to keep me in my place?

Maybe you haven't consciously voiced such explicit questions, but I'll bet they've shaped your view of God in some fashion. When you know you've sinned, do you assume God is sorry He saved you? Do you assume God loves others more than He loves you? Do you feel that you're a consistent failure in His eyes? Do you feel you need to obey to keep Him happy toward you? Do you keep watch on your spiritual disciplines with a feeling of dread?

My theology favors a strong view of God's sovereignty and providence, sometimes leaning a little too hard on our unworthiness as sinners to receive God's love and mercy. And I understand why the people in my theological circles orbit in this direction.

I've watched many professing Christians in American culture celebrate a soft, permissive form of love attributed to God that never corrects sin, that tolerates every form of disobedience, and requires zero repentance or holiness. That's *not* God's love. It's not biblical. God's love never allows us to continue in sin.[4] To be saved by grace through faith in Jesus will mean that we are sanctified—made holy—day by day as we walk in obedience to God's commands. He will shape our minds and hearts through Scripture, prayer, the church, and His Spirit. He never leaves us to continue living in sin. As the old hymn declares, we're "saved to sin no more!"[5]

Following Jesus requires repentance because true saving faith will change the way we live. Our former lives were characterized by sin and, if that wasn't a problem, then we wouldn't have needed Jesus to die for us and pay for our sin.

But sin *was* our problem, and we *did* need Jesus to free us from it.

God's love does not permit ongoing, unrepentant sin. That said, it is a massive overcorrection to reduce God's love to something so miserly that we're not even sure if God *likes* us. Twenty-five years ago, theologian Don Carson wrote *The Difficult Doctrine*

---

4. Among other texts, the book of 1 John speaks strongly to this.
5. "Praise for the Fountain Opened," by William Cowper, 1731–1800. Public domain.

of the Love of God in response to the growing theological trend that emphasized a permissive and theologically weak definition of God's love to the exclusion of His holiness and justice. Carson wrote, "Nowadays if you tell people that God loves them, they are unlikely to be surprised. Of course God loves me; he's like that, isn't he? Besides, why shouldn't he love me? I'm kind of cute, or at least as nice as the next person. I'm okay, you're okay, and God loves you and me."[6] Carson's book served as a needed correction in a day when Christians were tempted to extol God as a divine kind of Santa Claus who looked the other way when you were naughty.

To be certain, Carson's correction is still a needed word as we seek to keep our understanding of God's attributes balanced in our minds. In the years since, though, I think perhaps we've moved too far in the other direction, tipping again toward an imbalanced view of God's love as it pertains to God's holiness. It's difficult to grasp in human terms what God expresses perfectly without detracting from all His other perfect, divine attributes. He is able to be everything that He is perfectly, without compromising any part of His character. Carson says that God "enjoys all knowledge. He not only knows everything—he even knows what might have been under different circumstances . . . and takes that into account when he judges (Matt. 11:20–24) . . . God's knowledge is perfect."[7]

Psalm 139 helps us rightly understand God's perfect knowledge and investment in our lives. He doesn't know and ignore. He knows and loves. He places value on our lives as image bearers. He ordered our steps and ordained our days before He spoke the world into existence. He has always planned to save you, so your life will always matter to Him. Jesus said that God knows

6. D. A. Carson, *The Difficult Doctrine of the Love of God* (Crossway, 2000), 12.
7. Ibid., 50.

the number of hairs on your head.[8] If you're like me, that number varies wildly every day. Between shedding and regrowth, the number of hairs on my head is an ever-changing integer. He knows the number of hairs on your head too. And freckles and T cells and heartbeats. Why would He bother with that kind of knowledge if He didn't love us?

Yes, God is fully aware of our sinful state. The Bible is rife with truths about the condition of the human heart. God knows:

> "The heart is deceitful above all things, and desperately sick; who can understand it?" (Jer. 17:9)

> "And no creature is hidden from his sight, but all are naked and exposed to the eyes of him to whom we must give account." (Heb. 4:13)

> "But Jesus, knowing their thoughts, said, 'Why do you think evil in your hearts?'" (Matt. 9:4)

> "Every way of man is right in his own eyes, but the Lord weighs the heart." (Prov. 21:2)

> "None is righteous, no, not one; no one understands; no one seeks for God." (Rom. 3:10–11)

The Bible always tells the truth about our hearts. And because the Bible is God's Word, God is the one telling the truth about who we are. He knows who we really are. That's *why* He sent Jesus to die in our place to bear judgment for our sins. He loved us while we were still in our sinful condition and sent Jesus to rescue us.[9] This is real love. This is affection. It's not miserly or drudgery.

8. Matthew 10:30.
9. Romans 5:8.

It's not begrudging or disgruntled. God doesn't do anything He doesn't want to do. He cannot be coerced into loving us.[10] He just *does*. Because it delights Him to do so. Read that again. God *delighted* in saving you and making you a new creature in Christ. He was *happy* to provide a way out for you.

John Piper notes the many ways that God is happy in saving sinners:

> Luke 15, over and over, like four times, talks about gladness. "Just so, I tell you, there will be more joy in heaven over one sinner who repents than over ninety-nine righteous persons who need no repentance" (Luke 15:7). We know it's talking not just about the angels throwing a party, but God himself, because in the parable of the prodigal son, that's in fact what he does. He runs out. He grabs his son, hugs him, throws a party, and says, "Come on, come on, older son. He's home, he's alive!" I mean, this father is just oozing gladness, not begrudging, as if he is saying, "I guess I have to save my son who wrecked all my property." It's just not like that.[11]

If God oozes joy and gladness when you come to faith in Jesus, why would He suddenly change character and become a grump who stiff-arms you with His affection and delight? That's not God, my friend. He disciplines us when we sin, but He does not hold us in contempt.

Piper continues, "He never looks upon us with contempt because he's always for us, never against us. He will always restore

---

10. I'm indebted to John Piper for his book *The Pleasures of God*, which expounds on the idea that God is perfectly happy in and of Himself. He doesn't love us because He has to.
11. John Piper, "Is God Angry at Me When I Sin?," Desiring God, June 26, 2019, https://www.desiringgod.org/interviews/is-god-angry-at-me-when-i-sin.

us and bring us unfailingly to an eternity where there will be no grieving him, no quenching him, no displeasing him anymore."[12] It does not hold true with God's character for Him to move from someone who was happy to save you to someone who is grouchy about sanctifying you. He is not wishy-washy like we are. He doesn't change like we do. He doesn't come unhinged when we disobey. He is steady. Sure. Certain. Unfailing. Don't let *your* response to someone's disobedience color your picture of God's response. God is not like us. When His children disobey, He does correct. But He does not lose His mind with rage. He is measured in His responses; His wrath is not disproportionately imbalanced. And His wrath toward our sin was swallowed by His Son at the cross. And it was finished. *Enough*. It will always be enough.

THE GOD WHO LOVES YOU

"Even before a word is on my tongue, behold, O LORD, you know it altogether." Psalm 139:4 removes any doubt about God's insight into our hearts. He knows what we're going to think when someone criticizes us at work. He knows the words that will plume into the air before we form a response. He knows the shape of the vowels and consonants before they are formed by our mouths and tongues. He knows it altogether. And yet, because He sent Jesus, He is also the God who doesn't treat us as our sins deserve. Neither does He hold sin against us. He knows every scornful thought or angry word, but when we have believed in Jesus for forgiveness of sins, He doesn't dangle our sins over our heads so we'll live in perpetual regret and defeat. Rather, He loves you.

12. Piper, "Is God Angry at Me When I Sin?"

The link between knowledge and love is a biblical one. There are eleven variants or synonyms for the word *know* in Psalm 139. They connote closeness, intimacy, personal care. David's psalm about God's knowledge of us is consistent with all of Scripture. In the New Testament, Paul writes about God's foreknowledge in regard to those who would believe in Jesus for salvation and forgiveness of sins. Known as "The Golden Chain," Paul links our certain position as children of God to His love for us: "For those whom he foreknew he also predestined to be conformed to the image of his Son, in order that he might be the firstborn among many brothers. And those whom he predestined he also called, and those whom he called he also justified, and those whom he justified he also glorified" (Rom. 8:29–30).

When you let all of Scripture speak to you of who God is, then you begin to see how God can both know and love.

The word *foreknew* doesn't come across in English the way it does in the original text. As in Psalm 139, the Old Testament writers used a word for *know* that implies personal interest, investment, care. In keeping with that, Paul also uses a word that communicates love.[13] Fore*knew* means fore*loved*. Essentially, Paul is saying God set His affections on those He would save before they ever existed. Before the universe itself existed![14] This is God's knowledge. This is God's love. Not a meaningless accumulation of facts.

God knows and loves us, and He is not repelled by the ones He saved by grace through faith.

---

13. I'm grateful for John Stott's helpful explanation of this passage. John Stott, *The Message of Romans* (InterVarsity Press, 1994), 249.
14. Ephesians 1:3–10.

David, our author of Psalm 139, also penned Psalm 103. When you let all of Scripture speak to you of who God is, then you begin to see how God can both know *and* love. David wrote: "As a father shows compassion to his children, so the LORD shows compassion to those who fear him. For he knows our frame; he remembers that we are dust" (Ps. 103:13–14). God knows we are weak, and He has compassion for us. Compassion is never disgruntled. Compassion moves one to act on behalf of someone else. That's what God has done for us!

"He does not deal with us according to our sins, nor repay us according to our iniquities. For as high as the heavens are above the earth so great is his steadfast love toward those who fear him; as far as the east is from the west, so far does he remove our transgressions from us" (Ps. 103:10–12). He has lovingly made a way for you to be forgiven and made new, to remove the stain of sin, to clothe you in the righteousness of Jesus. He wouldn't do that so that He could then treat you as your sins *do* deserve. God didn't save us so He could hold us at arm's length to remind us how wretched we are. We're not wretched anymore. We're sons and daughters.

KNOWN AND NOT DESPISED

God knows you to the core. And He loves you anyway. If you have believed in Jesus for salvation, you have been moved from enemy to friend, hostile to holy, far off to very near. His love changes you. His love is making you what you need to be. God knew you when you were an enemy, and His love has made you a friend. A son, a daughter, an heir of all that He has. God did not happily save you to then reluctantly sanctify you. That lavish love in saving you is still present in your sanctification.

God is too happy in Himself and His glory to be brought low in attitude. He's not like us. He is constant and true, steady and unchanging in regard to you. We may leave His path, but He never leaves ours.[15] We may vary in the temperature of our affections, but He never does. In Christ, you are known and not despised.

Jesus came to reveal the Father to us, to give us access to Him without fear or shame. He bore our sins in His body on the cross so that we might die to sin and live to righteousness.[16] He removed the curse of sin by becoming sin for us and giving us His righteousness. This was always God's plan in saving us. Before galaxies, your salvation. Before the universe, your sanctification.

When Jesus walked the earth, He often spoke about how He was known and loved by the Father, how they were united in will and love. We are tempted to read our Bibles and think that Jesus is the kindest person of the Trinity, that He is holding back the Father's wrath. But that's neither truthful nor fair. Jesus radiated the glory of the Father to us. He was the *exact* imprint of His nature.[17] We see Jesus' compassion toward the people He taught and healed, and we somehow separate that from the Father's heart. But no. Jesus' compassion for us mirrors the Father's compassion for us.

Jesus said, "I am the good shepherd. I know my own and my own know me, just as the Father knows me and I know the Father; and I lay down my life for the sheep" (John 10:14–15). He knows us and loves us. Through Jesus, the Father has brought us into His family. He's changed us. Sinner to saint. Far to near. Enemy to friend. Exile to heir.

---

15. A rephrased quote from Charles Spurgeon, *Treasury of David: A Commentary on the Psalms*, "Psalm 139" (Hendrickson Publishers, 1876), 222. "I may leave thy path, but you never leave mine."
16. 1 Peter 2:24.
17. Hebrews 1:3.

We belong to Him. So, we can live for Him. Because we are loved by Him.

○ ○ ○

for further thought:

1. If God knows every single thing about you, how does the idea of being so exposed make you feel?

2. What do you learn about God's character from Psalm 139:1–4?

3. If you have struggled to believe that God freely gives His love and does not falter in His affections for you, how can you find comfort from Psalm 103:10–14?

4. How does Jesus show us who the Father is and how He thinks about us?

5. When you are tempted to believe that God loves you less than He did when He saved you, what truths from Scripture can help you rightly view His steadfast, unchanging nature? Write them down and commit to memorizing one or two of them.

"O LORD, you have searched me and known me!
You know when I sit down and when I rise up;
    you discern my thoughts from afar.
You search out my path and my lying down
    and are acquainted with all my ways.
Even before a word is on my tongue,
    behold, O LORD, you know it altogether."

PSALM
139:5–6

You hem me in, behind and before,
    and lay your hand upon me.
Such knowledge is too wonderful for me;
it is high; I cannot attain it.

2

Known and Safe

Why Can't I Know Everything?

When I think about my childhood, I think about my mother's hands. I picture her at the stove, her hand stirring a pot of soup or holding a spatula while browning meat for spaghetti. I see her hands scrubbing down bathroom counters and pulling weeds in the flowerbed. I remember her sitting with her Bible in her lap in the mornings, a pen in her left hand and coffee in her right. Blue-veined with squared joints from severe arthritis, my mother's hands hold many of my memories.

Mostly, though, I remember her hands on my face when I was sick. She rarely used a thermometer, but a gentle press of her hands across a forehead could instantly diagnose a fever. I remember her cool hands on my face, the way I'd instinctively close my eyes when she pressed her palm against my forehead and the back of her knuckles across my cheeks. Ever gentle in her touch, I felt safe when my mom laid her hand on me.

I find myself mothering like her. I always check the forehead first, then the cheeks because she taught me that foreheads are always hot, but a true fever will warm the cheeks as well. My boys react much as I did, eyes sliding shut as I gently feel their faces for warmth. When they were little, I curled around them in their beds, my hand on their cheek, making sure they knew that Mom wouldn't leave until they felt better. Squished together in a twin bed, I would press in and feel them lean into me in their sleep. There's comfort in being pushed in close to the one who makes you feel safe.

THE ONE WHO IS FAITHFULLY PRESENT

Psalm 139 gives us a layered look at God's character and, though He is far more than any one attribute, verse 5 explores His presence as He presses in close to His people. "You hem me in, behind and before," the psalmist writes, painting a picture of God's intentional nearness. We're surrounded on all sides by His presence: behind and before. *Hemmed in.*

Translations vary in their approach to the word used in verse 5 to describe this hemming in. Some lean toward a military analogy, others a tightknit closeness. *Encircled, hemmed, enclosed, hedged, beset,* and (my personal favorite) *squeezed in.* I see reassurance in every synonym. This enclosure is meant to be a comfort, a presence felt and recognized. On the heels of a description of God's intimate acquaintance with our thoughts, habits, actions, sleep patterns, and words comes the phrase that marries His knowledge with His care: *You hem me in, You encircle me, You enclose me, You beset me, You squeeze me in.* The definition for the Hebrew word here includes the word "cramped."[1] The picture we get is the Lord coming in close to both protect and prevent escape. Is this a comfort or a threat? Should we fear God being so near and so close with His presence? David follows

---

1. "H6696 - ṣûr," Strong's Hebrew Lexicon (ESV), Blue Letter Bible, https://www.blueletterbible.org/lexicon/h6696/esv/wlc/0-1/.

up with a reassuring phrase: "you lay your hand upon me."

If you've ever struggled to believe that God is intimately involved in your personal life, this phrase is proof positive that He is. If you have believed in Jesus for forgiveness of your sins, you belong to God. You are known. You are loved. You are *His*. And He doesn't walk away from those upon whom He has set His steadfast love. He is so involved in your life that He rests His hand upon you. No, not physically. (This is a metaphor, of course.) But what my mother's hands communicated in her fingers upon my forehead is the kind of staying, faithful, present love that God communicates in promising His presence.[2] His hand is a picture of comfort, guidance, safety, love, *presence*. He has promised to be with you, and He is faithfully sticking it out. He's there for the long haul, working out His good purposes in your life.[3]

For the Christian, God's nearness isn't a threat. It's the deepest comfort we could ask for. When you wake up in the middle of the night in fear or anxiety, He is there, sovereignly ruling and holding you fast.[4] When you've sinned and cry out to Him to forgive, He is there to forgive.[5] When your heart feels cold or dry, He is there to awaken your affections through His Word.[6] When you aren't sure what to do, He is there to give you wisdom anytime you ask.[7] When you're lonely, He is your faithful friend.[8] When you're wandering away from His side, He is there

---

2. I've written a book on the theme and promise of God's presence as an expression of His steadfast love. Check out *The Promise Is His Presence: Why God Is Always Enough* for an in-depth look at God's presence from Genesis to Revelation.
3. Philippians 1:6.
4. Isaiah 41:10.
5. 1 John 1:9.
6. Psalm 34:8.
7. James 1:5.
8. Psalm 25:14.

to correct and bring you back.[9] When you are grieved and afraid, He is with you in the valley of the shadow of death.[10]

God communicates His steadfast love by being present with us. He sent Jesus—Immanuel—to be God with us. Our future home in heaven is called Jehovah Shammah, which means *the Lord is there*—for the true gift of heaven is God Himself.[11] He knows that nothing satisfies or brings us peace like being pressed in, encircled, enclosed, or squeezed in by Him. His steadfast love is better than anything this life has to offer and stronger than anything this life throws at us. When you are overwhelmed by your circumstances, your sin, your shortcomings—He is there. And He is enough to help you endure, stand firm, obey, and follow Him in faithfulness.

> God is inclined toward *His people,* not away from them. He loves them by hemming them in, by laying His hand upon them.

If it's hard to remember that God is near, I'd like to challenge you to try an exercise that I believe will awaken your heart to His persistent promise of presence. Choose a book of the Bible. I suggest starting with Psalms or the gospel of John. Over the next few months, work slowly through the book, reading small portions each day and answering one question: *What do I learn about God from this passage?* Get a notebook and a pen and write out what you find each day. If the text lists His character traits, write that down. If it talks about things He has done, write that down. If you see Him orchestrating and working things together in the background of a story, write that down.

9. Psalm 32:4–5.
10. Psalm 23:4.
11. Ezekiel 48:35.

I embarked on this very challenge more than a decade ago and through careful study of God's character in the Bible, my theology was demolished and rebuilt. I worked through much of the Bible answering this one question, and I learned that God is inclined *toward* His people, not away from them. He loves them by hemming them in, by laying His hand upon them. Like the comforting hands of my mother when my fever raged, God's nearness is a balm that binds you up with healing. He presses in because He loves you. He has dealt with your sin and He has made you His own. Rather than keeping Himself from you while you scramble to get your act together, He is invested in your life, teaching, correcting, guiding, and growing you in faith. Enjoy His comforting presence. Take confidence in knowing that your sin was paid for at the cross and Jesus has made it possible for you to draw near to the Father without fear.[12] You are delightfully hemmed in.

THE ONE WHO IS INFINITELY KNOWLEDGEABLE

When you consider all the things that God knows and the way He is always present, it's a bit much to take in. That's where David goes in verse 6: "Such knowledge is too wonderful for me; it is high; I cannot attain it." God's omniscience (being all-knowing) is one of His attributes that sets Him apart from us. While we desire to know everything, He actually *does* know everything. He didn't have to learn things like we must. He just *knows*.

The apostle Paul echoes David's sentiments in his doxology in Romans 11:

Oh, the depth of the riches of the wisdom and the knowledge of God! How unsearchable are his judgments and how

---

12. Hebrews 10:19–20.

inscrutable his ways! "For who has known the mind of the Lord, or who has been his counselor?" "Or who has given a gift to him that he might be repaid?" For from him and through him and to him are all things. To him be glory forever. Amen. (Rom. 11:33–36)

God's knowledge is infinite, immeasurable, unsearchable. We can't know all that He knows, no matter how desperately we try.

PURSUING KNOWLEDGE TO CONTROL OUTCOMES

I was born in 1981. The internet didn't make its way into our home until I was in the eighth grade, and when it did, it was the dial-up kind you could only use if the telephone land line wasn't in use. (It pains me to know that some of you younger readers won't know what I'm talking about.) Up until the day I learned how to fire up AOL on our big, clunky desktop computer, if there was something I wanted to know, I went to my dad's home office, pulled one of those cream and dark green encyclopedias off his bookshelf, and thumbed through it until I found what I was looking for. *What is a leap year?* Go to the L volume. *Is a penguin a bird or an amphibian?* Open the P volume. And if I didn't find what I was looking for, then it was simply unknowable. I could ask my parents or wait for a trip to the library to peruse their books, but there was a lot in life I had to be content not to know.

Being content with a lack of knowledge is nearly maddening today, though. We live in a culture where knowledge is currency—and we are filthy rich. Anytime there is a natural disaster, an act of violence, or a politically newsworthy story, we race to our search engines to stalk the story until we are satisfied with what we've learned. If we're not satisfied, we remain glued to our devices, haunting the news sites or social media apps until we know as much as humanly possible. The truth is we'd like to know *more* than what is humanly possible, and we're closer to that unattainable goal as anyone in history has ever been able to come.

With the advent of the internet and then smartphones, we can acquire knowledge with a swipe, a tap, or a voice command. Siri, or her Amazon counterpart, Alexa, tells us everything we want to know. We think having more knowledge will bring us more peace and contentment, but the more knowledge we seek to acquire, the more frazzled and anxious we seem to become. Jen Wilkin writes, "Our insatiable desire for information is a clear sign that we covet the divine omniscience. We want all the facts, but as finite beings we are not designed to have them. And so, not surprisingly, unmeasured consumption of information brings us not increased peace of mind, as we had hoped, but increased dissonance."[13]

We think having more knowledge will bring us more peace and contentment, but the more knowledge we seek to acquire, the more frazzled and anxious we seem to become.

This is an old problem—the first problem, actually. Think back to the garden of Eden. When Satan tempted Adam and Eve to eat from the tree of the knowledge of good and evil, he told them that eating of the tree would make them like God, *knowing* good and evil.[14] In a desire to have godlike knowledge, Adam and Eve disobeyed and brought the curse of sin upon themselves. They wanted to know what God knows but were not

---

13. Jen Wilkin, *None Like Him: 10 Ways God Is Different from Us (and Why That's a Good Thing)* (Crossway, 2016), 111.
14. See Genesis 3:5.

created with the capacity to hold that kind of knowledge.

Thousands of years later, we too long for the trait of omniscience, often living as though we already *have* God's limitless knowledge. We presume to know what others are thinking, assigning motive without proof. We make decisions based on how we feel rather than what might actually be true. We replace prayer with search engines, fusing together our trust in God with all the research the internet might produce. But is it really trust when you have all the answers? Does your constant search for knowledge bring true peace and trust in the Lord? Or does it fuel your anxiety as you second-guess every decision?

I am an expert in researching health symptoms. In my early years of dealing with various autoimmune disorders, I employed Dr. Google to help me feel in control of my health. There's nothing wrong with research, right? And knowledge is power! But the deeper I went down the rabbit hole of research, the more I began to feel like I was on the other side of Alice's looking glass—desperate for peace I could not reach. My constant googling ramped up my anxiety by leaps and bounds. My husband eventually asked me to stop searching health conditions online because my anxiety was affecting my sleep, my spiritual life, and our relationship. Nothing was as it seemed. Knowledge wasn't power. It was paranoia. A bug bite had to be cancer. A dehydration headache was probably a brain tumor. Indigestion was definitely a heart attack. Basically, everything Google said was wrong with me was out to kill me.

I didn't realize it, but I was trying to be like God in how much I knew. I thought my pursuit of knowledge would make me feel empowered, and sometimes it did. But my inability to stop trying to control everything with my newfound knowledge left me frazzled, anxious, and fearful. It's not the knowledge itself that's the problem. It's what we *do* with it. And what we do with knowledge is obsessively try to control outcomes. I think this is partly why God forbade the tree of the knowledge of good and evil in the garden—because what we do in our pursuit of omniscience quickly morphs into idolatry. Control. Manipulation. If we have all the knowledge, then *we* are the masters of our destiny. Or so we like to think.

The psalmist reorients us to what is true: God's knowledge is limitless, and we cannot fathom or attain it. Nor should we try. Verse 6 is a line in the sand, dividing the Creator from the created. He is God and we are not. We cannot know everything, nor were we made to live and function while knowing everything. Omniscience is a divine trait, not a human one. But our finite limitations are not necessarily a curse. Our limitations keep us close to the Lord, desperate for His care, His intervention, His sovereign control. Anything that keeps us close to Him is a gift. It's freeing! We don't have to try to control every outcome, hedge every bet, prepare for every possible disaster. We trust a God who sits on His throne and no plan of His can be thwarted.[15] He created everything and He rules over everything. This is the God who knows you, saved you, loves you, is *with* you. The One who knows everything that will ever happen to you hems you in with His presence and love.

> *Our finite limitations keep us close to the Lord. Anything that keeps us close to Him is a gift.*

THE ONE WHO KNOWS IS NEAR

There's a correlation between knowledge and fear. It's good for us to learn, grow, and try new things. I'm a voracious reader, and

---

15. Job 42:2.

I love to research places and people I read about. I enjoy podcasts about strange stories from history, and I'm always interested in learning how to better my sourdough baking skills. I love to listen to a good sermon, read my Bible early in the morning, discuss what I'm learning with other believers. We will always be learning new things about the Lord as we follow Him. In fact, we're commanded in Scripture to grow in grace and knowledge of Jesus.[16] Learning is a part of the Christian life! But our growth in knowledge of God shouldn't lead us to try to live apart from Him. And that is what the desire for omniscience does—it pulls us away from our dependence on Him and seeks to put ourselves in His place.

The One who knows all rules all. That should be a comfort to us when we are fearful about what might happen.

No matter how much research we can dig up on a troubling issue, we can't control the outcome because we are human. We do not have the omnipotence to go along with omniscience. But God does. In addition to His strength and knowledge, He is also good. And that means we can trust Him with our scariest scenarios, our deepest fears, our most crippling anxieties.

In embracing our limitations as finite beings, we can acknowledge and worship God for His sovereign control and limitless knowledge. The One who knows all rules all. That should be a comfort to us when we are fearful about what *might* happen. In Colossians, Paul says that in Jesus "all things hold together" (Col. 1:17). The author of Hebrews similarly says, "He upholds the universe by the word of his power" (Heb. 1:3).

---

16. 2 Peter 3:18.

Picture this: Jesus is holding the universe in His hands. Remember that song from Sunday school that declared "He's got the whole world in His hands"? The sentiment is right, if incomplete. He does have the whole world in His hands. He also has the whole *universe* in His hands. There isn't a planet rotating outside of its orbit without His command because Jesus is holding the universe together. There's not a circumstance in your life that is spinning out of His control, because Jesus is holding the universe together. What you have in Christ is perfect, complete knowledge—plus perfect, complete power, plus perfect, complete goodness. He acts in ways that are good and for our best because He knows and sees all, and because His actions are not tainted by sin or selfishness. He is in control and that's a good thing. He's trustworthy.

When we couple Psalm 139:5–6 with the previous four verses, we get a clearer picture of who God is to us. He knows everything about us—every thought, every word, every action, every motive. He has ordained all our days and will bring about His good purposes in our lives. Rather than creating us and walking away, leaving us to fend for ourselves, He is near, invested, present. He surrounds us with His presence, hemming us in. Enclosed, encircled. Squeezed in. He lays His hand upon us, guiding us, comforting us, protecting us. He won't leave or forsake us. His knowledge is limitless; it's beyond our comprehension.

If God is described in these ways, can't we trust Him with our lives? Rather than frantically trying to protect ourselves with the pseudo armor of intellect and search engine results, can't we remember that He lays His hand upon us?

These first six verses of Psalm 139 speak to our anxious fears. When we acknowledge our inability to control the outcome of our circumstances, we are free to trust the One who *does* know it all and who *is* in control of the outcome. This doesn't mean He won't allow you to experience suffering. Sometimes the weight of His hand upon you is heavy with grief or sorrow or pain. Sometimes His hand holds sufferings for you that will produce the fruit of perseverance. It is the way of the Christian life to suffer, for we follow a Savior who suffered.

But our Savior is also kind and good. And He will not waste the sorrows we feel this side of heaven. Rather, He will use them to prepare us for heaven.[17] We have trusted Him with our eternity, and we can trust Him with today. As the psalmist writes, "Be still, and know that I am God" (Ps. 46:10). Stop striving. You are not producing anything good while striving to control. Remember that God is God, and you are not. And be freed from the temptation to think you must hold all things together. Only He does that. And He's very good at it.

KNOWN AND SAFE

Most of the things that send me on a rampage of anxious strivings are based in fear. Health concerns, wondering if my kids will turn out okay, financial strains. Most of the time, my fear is rooted in doubt of God's ability to hold me fast. What I want is a guarantee of a trouble-free existence for me and my family. What I get from Scripture is a promise that God will win in the end.

So for now, my calling and yours is to cease striving because we weren't meant to hold all things together. Not even the things in our own personal little orbits. God knows every detail. He is neither surprised by the past nor unprepared for the future, for He has written the ending to your story already. While I cannot promise you a physically safe, trouble-free existence, I *can* promise you that in Christ your heart is eternally safe. There is

---

17. 2 Corinthians 4:17

nothing that can happen on this earth that can tear you from the God who hems you in with His presence. Hands open, friend. Your white-knuckled grip on things won't lead you to peace and trust. But confidence in His presence, which He has promised in His Word, *will*. Your frenzied drive to know everything you possibly can won't help you fix your broken circumstances. But fixing your eyes on the One who holds the universe in His hands will help you to navigate them with joy.

Open your Bible. Look for what you learn about this God who knows and sees and presses in close. Write down every trait, every attribute, every word that tells you He is near. Feel His hand on your cheek. He knows you. He is with you. Your heart is safe.

○ ○ ○

for further thought:

1. What do you learn about God's character in Psalm 139:5–6?

2. How can the truth that God hems you in encourage you when you are afraid or lonely or uncertain?

3. Read Hebrews 10:19–22. Should we fear the presence of God? Why or why not?

4. Is the relentless pursuit of knowledge an idol in your life? How might it prevent you from growing your trust in God?

5. List the ways that you see God's promise to be with His people throughout the story of Scripture.

Where shall I go from your Spirit?
　　Or where shall I flee from your presence?
If I ascend to heaven, you are there!
If I make my bed in Sheol, you are there!
If I take the wings of the morning
　　and dwell in the uttermost parts of the sea,
even there your hand shall lead me,
　　and your right hand shall hold me.
If I say, "Surely the darkness shall cover me,
　　and the light about me be night,"
even the darkness is not dark to you;
　　the night is bright as the day,
　　for darkness is as light with you.

3

Known When You Want to Run

What if I'm Too Ashamed to Face God?

I am a homebody. I am happiest in my little house in my little town with my little family. Ironically, I am also a person who travels a fair bit for work. I spend at least one weekend a month in a new city by myself, and I'm usually counting down the hours until I'm home.

Once I've settled into my hotel after a day of air travel, I check the map on my phone to see how far away I am from my family. My husband, teenage son, and I all share a GPS app for safety reasons, and when I open that map, I feel a pang of homesickness when I see the geographical distance between us. There's nothing like waking up in a Hampton Inn fifteen hundred miles from home to make you feel lonely. I can never shake how isolated I feel when I'm sprinting through airports alone, eating alone, fixing my coffee alone in the hotel lobby. But I always cheer myself with the truth that I'm not actually alone. Wherever I go, the Lord is there.

WHEREVER I GO . . .

In verses 7–10 of Psalm 139, David employs a literary device to illustrate the transcendence of God's presence. He asks, "Where shall I go from your Spirit? Or where shall I flee from your presence?" He answers his own question by comparing two sets of opposites, showing us the inescapable reach of God. "If I ascend to heaven, you are there! If I make my bed in Sheol, you are there!" David isn't referring to heaven and hell as we think of them through the lens of New Testament teaching. Sheol here refers to the grave or the place of the dead.

"If I take the wings of the morning and dwell in the uttermost parts of the sea, even there your hand shall lead me, and your right hand shall hold me." Here, he's comparing the "wings of the morning"—what we think of as sunrise—with the "far side of the sea"—the far western edge of the Mediterranean Sea, past the known world of that time, into the sunset. Imagine David pointing up and down (north and south), and then panning his arm from side to side (east to west). No matter where you go, God is there. He takes up all the room in the universe! And though David couldn't imagine man walking on the moon or hurtling through space like an astronaut, God is there, too, holding space with the stars He has named.[1]

This kind of presence means something for us. Remember, God isn't *passively* knowledgeable. Neither is He passively present. His omniscience and omnipresence are divine qualities that have bearing on our lives. God isn't frantically tracking my flight and hoping I arrive safely. The pairing of His knowledge with His presence *determines* the outcome of my days. While I can

---

1. Psalm 147:4.

use the GPS feature on my phone to see where my husband and sons are while I'm out of town, I can't *determine* what happens to them. God's knowledge is "qualitatively different from ours. For example, our knowledge is not determinative of reality. Our knowing that apples are red does not make them red. The Lord's knowledge, however, does determine reality."[2]

God's knowledge means something deeper than ours. And paired with His omnipresence, our lives are safely held by His hands. There's nowhere you can go where He is not, and there's nothing that can happen to you without His say-so. These verses urge us to take comfort in God's protective presence.

We cannot geographically hide from God. We know this. But still, we hide sometimes. Or try to. Whether we call it an existential hiding or a spiritual sprint away from Him, there are times when we hold the Lord at arm's length, keeping our hearts from Him as if He doesn't already know what we're cramming into the darkest corners of our souls. As if He hadn't seen this day long before He divided time into days and nights. Tim Keller calls it relational running—hiding from the face of God.[3] What makes us run? What makes us turn off the lights so no one sees what we're trying to hide? Shame. Shame for sin in the past, shame for sin from this morning. Pre-conversion sins. Post-conversion sins. We hide what we're ashamed of, what we think makes us unredeemable and unlovable. The good news is that there is nowhere to run from God. The better news is that there's no reason to run from Him at all.

2. Ligonier, "Our All-Knowing, All-Seeing Lord," March 18, 2015, https://www
   .ligonier.org/learn/devotionals/our-all-knowing-all-seeing-lord.
3. Dr. Timothy Keller, "Running From God," a sermon from Jonah 1:1–10, preached
   at Redeemer Presbyterian Church on September 9, 2001, https://podcast.gospelin
   life.com/e/running-from-god/.

HIDING THE SINS OF YESTERDAY

When Adam and Eve first sinned, they hid from God. Stitching together fig leaves to cover their bodies and their shame, they sought to shield themselves from what they had to know was coming. *Confrontation.* When God called out "Where are you?" it wasn't as if He didn't know.[4] His question was meant to draw them out and reveal their sin. Shame is the first consequence we feel for sin, and rightly so. Sin is an offense to God that pollutes our relationship with Him. If we feel *no* shame over sin, we should be worried. Paul tells us that hard, callous hearts feel no shame over sin, resulting in lifestyles characterized by blatant, unrepentant disobedience.[5] The initial feeling of shame should send us sprinting toward our Savior for forgiveness in repentance. But what we often do with shame is give it a soapbox. We forge our identities in the fires of what we have done rather than what Jesus has done for us.

This kind of shame condemns and lies. It convinces us we can never be right with God.

This kind of soul-crushing shame makes us want to hide, makes us want to cover our sin and our tracks, to distance ourselves from the thing we're embarrassed about *and* the One who has never done anything shameful. This kind of shame makes you want to hide from Jesus when you remember what you did, turning you *away* from Christ rather than *to* Him. This kind of shame condemns and lies. It convinces us we can never be right with God, that we cannot be truly loved, that on some level, God will always, always be angry at us. This kind of shame tells us we can never come home again to our Savior.

4. Genesis 3:9.
5. Ephesians 4:19.

Our response to our sin should never be to run from Jesus. Rather, we should always run *to* Him. Run to Him and sin no more.

SIN NO MORE

When Jesus confronted the woman caught in adultery in John 8, her sin was shamefully exposed for all to see. She was caught *in the act* of adultery, and though our conservative sensibilities want to gloss over what that means when we read the text, it means exactly what you think it means. She was caught in the act. According to Old Testament law, both she and the man she was with should be put to death.[6] While the religious leaders gathered around the adulterous woman to stone her, Jesus rebuked them saying, "Let him who is without sin among you be the first to throw a stone at her" (John 8:7). It began to dawn on those in the crowd how unqualified they were to stone her and, beginning with those who were older, they dispersed. Then Jesus spoke to her alone. "'Woman, where are they? Has no one condemned you?' She said, 'No one, Lord.' And Jesus said, 'Neither do I condemn you; go, and from now on sin no more'" (John 8:10–11).[7]

> The stench of sin evaporates as you don the purity and holiness of Christ.

In one encounter with Jesus, this woman's shame and condemnation were removed and she was charged to live her life without sinning in this way again. This is what Jesus does for us

---

6. Deuteronomy 22:22.
7. Though early manuscripts of the gospel of John do not include this portion of John 8, the principle is not out of step with the overall teaching of Scripture in general or with Jesus during His earthly ministry in particular. Most scholars believe John 7:53–8:11 to be canonical, even if the author wasn't John himself.

when we come to faith for the first time. He awakens our dead hearts, gives us faith to believe that He is the Son of God and that He gave His life to pay for our sins, and He makes us completely new. John says that if we confess our sins, God is faithful and just to forgive and cleanse us from all unrighteousness.[8]

When we believe in Jesus for forgiveness of sins, a beautiful exchange occurs. Jesus, who never sinned, *became* our sin in our place on the cross.[9] He took all our shame, all our disobedience, our rebellion, our pride, our sexual sins, our selfishness, our idolatry, drunkenness, gluttony, envy, anger—He took it all as His own on the cross. *His life for ours.* And where God used to look at us and see all our sinfulness, He now sees the purity of Jesus because we are now clothed with His righteousness. Shame is washed away in the blood of Jesus. The stench of sin evaporates as you don the purity and holiness of Christ. The theological term for this is *imputed righteousness.* You are dressed in His goodness. All the condemnation you rightly deserved for your sin was swallowed by Jesus at the cross. There's none left for you anymore.[10]

When you think about all the shameful things you did before the Lord saved you, consider this from Colossians:

> And you who were dead in your trespasses and the uncircumcision of your flesh, God made alive together with him, having forgiven us all our trespasses, by canceling the record of debt that stood against us with its legal demands. This he set aside, nailing it to the cross. (Col. 2:13–14)

All those ugly things—those hostile, unholy, selfish, perverted, immoral, shameful thoughts and words and actions—*forgiven.*

8. 1 John 1:9.
9. 2 Corinthians 5:21.
10. Romans 8:1.

The record of debt you accrued for your life of sin—*canceled.* The shame you should feel for things that Jesus has taken upon His body to the cross—*removed.* But before the shame was removed, it was carried by Jesus who "endured the cross, despising the shame, and is seated at the right hand of the throne of God" (Heb. 12:2).

You and I both deserved to be nailed to the cross, to suffer for our sin, to bear God's righteous wrath, to endure the humiliation of public exposure for sins we have committed. But Jesus did this instead for sins He did *not* commit. "God's grace abolishes guilt forever."[11] Your shame has been removed by the Savior who loved you enough to take it upon Himself.

So don't wear it. Don't run back to shame and slip it over your shoulders like a garment that doesn't fit anymore. You're better dressed now than you could ever imagine. "Go and sin no more," Jesus says to us when we first believe and are forgiven. There's no need to hide your past sins from Him. He bled for them. He died for them. He was raised to free you from them. He already knows the things you are ashamed of, and what's more—He chooses to forget them.

God's knowledge, as we have discussed, is vaster and wider than we can fathom. But one thing He chooses to relinquish from the depths of His eternal memory is the remembrance of our sin. The psalmist writes: "For as high as the heavens are above the earth, so great is his steadfast love toward those who fear him; as far as the east is from the west, so far does he remove our transgressions from us" (Ps. 103:11–12). Again, it's that imagery of looking out as far as you can in the distance like in Psalm 139:7–10, but this time its fathoms and leagues of forgiveness that He puts between us and our sin.

11. Timothy Keller, *Rediscovering Jonah: The Secret of God's Mercy* (Penguin Books, 2018), 211.

If you come to God with perpetual feelings of shame, consider how He sees you according to Scripture. He is your Father. Not a father who is impatient and snippy and disgruntled with His children, but a father who "shows compassion to those who fear him. For he remembers our frame; he remembers that we are dust" (Ps. 103:13–14). He understands your frailty. And He doesn't hate you for it.[12]

If you have confessed your sin, believed in Jesus for forgiveness, and have been made alive in Christ, shame does not belong to you anymore. Jesus has removed your reproach by taking it upon Himself. If the voice you hear condemns you for sin that Jesus has paid for, that voice does not belong to the Lord. Run from it. Run *to* Jesus, instead.

Your shame for past sin was dealt with at the cross. God knew about it. He took care of it. It is finished. And if it is finished, you are free.

HIDING THE SINS OF TODAY

Maybe you read that last section and thought "That's not me. My worst sins were committed as a Christian." I understand that better than you might think. I was saved as a child. I have lived 84 percent of my life as a born-again believer in Jesus. (I did the math.) That means that most of my disobedience to God has occurred and will occur as a Christian who has been raised to new life in Christ. I must combat shame for post-conversion sins the way other Christians have to fight shame for pre-conversion sins. And shame has a different voice when you're a Christian.

If shame sounds condemning all the time, you question the genuineness of your faith as a Christian. "You profess to love

12. Psalm 69:33.

Jesus and you did *that?*" it says. "You're still doing *that* after you supposedly have been made a new creature in Christ?" The accusations ring true to us because we feel like we should be further along than we are, that we shouldn't be sinning like this anymore, that if Jesus had really changed us, we would be better than this.

One of my sons really wrestled with this issue when he first came to faith in Christ. When confronted with blatant disobedience, he would cry and say, "I'm not a Christian anymore!" He thought if he were truly saved, he wouldn't sin again. And though he was young in the faith when he had this thought, I know believers who have walked faithfully with Jesus for decades but still feel condemnation when they sin. Thankfully, God's Word addresses ongoing sin in the life of the believer and what to do about it. Hiding in shame isn't mentioned, I'd like to point out. Neither is living in fear that God hates you because you can't get your act together. On the contrary, you should run to Jesus. *Run.*

> This is what I deserve, you think, because I keep sinning. This is condemning yourself where God does not.

John writes,

> My little children, I am writing these things to you so that you may not sin. *But if anyone does sin,* we have an advocate with the Father, Jesus Christ the righteous. He is the propitiation for our sins, and not for ours only but also for the sins of the whole world. And by this we know that we have come to know him, if we keep his commandments. Whoever says, "I know him" but does not keep his commandments is a liar, and the truth is not in him, but

whoever keeps his word, in him truly the love of God is perfected. By this we may know that we are in him: whoever says he abides in him ought to walk in the same way in which he walked. (1 John 2:1–6)

Now, it's likely your eyes were immediately drawn to the "does not keep his commandments is a liar" part. As judge and jury, you've sentenced yourself to living as the Lord's least favorite child from here unto eternity. *This is what I deserve,* you think, *because I keep sinning. I keep lusting, overeating, losing my temper, getting jealous, cursing, lying, being lazy. God saved me but He gets to treat me like a second-class Christian because I am a second-class Christian.* This, my friend, is a joyless existence. This is self-flagellation. It's condemning yourself where God does not.

Many of us practice a form of penance when we sin, even if we don't call it that. We might punish ourselves by reading the Bible more or cutting something we enjoy from our diets for a while. We might keep an ongoing internal dialogue that berates and belittles ourselves. We might recuse ourselves from serving in church or taking part in a Bible study because we "don't deserve it." But here's where we must not confuse consequence with punishment. There are consequences for sin, and we must bear them. But punishing yourself for sin makes a theological statement about Jesus' finished work at the cross. Punishing yourself declares that your sins needed more than what Christ provided. Self-flagellation accomplishes nothing in the life of a Christian. It cannot pay for sin that Jesus has already paid for, and it is of no use in fighting temptation.[13]

Let's look at John's words a little more closely. His desire is that we do not sin. And that should be our desire, too. His

13. Colossians 2:23.

encouragements from 1 John 1 should turn our hearts to the superiority and divinity of Christ and to live fully with Him. Walk in the light, he tells us, with Jesus. These exhortations are meant to encourage us to live far from sin. But "if anyone does sin," John hedges, because he knows that we *will* sin, "we have an advocate with the Father, Jesus Christ the righteous" (2:1). John calls his Savior "Jesus Christ the righteous." Immediately, I picture Jesus on a white horse coming in to save the day—like King Richard the Lionhearted or Constantine the Great. Except Jesus really *is* the Savior on the white horse—as John will later tell us in Revelation—the Savior who will set all things right for good.[14]

What about the sins you've committed as a believer? Covered. His sacrifice is enough for your sin. All of your sin—past, present, future.

Jesus Christ the Righteous has not only died to free you from sin, He also lives to intercede for you.[15] He is our advocate, and He is the "propitiation" for our sin, John says. He has shielded you from God's righteous wrath toward your sin by absorbing judgment for you. John also says that Jesus' blood is enough to cover the sins of the whole world. Though not everyone will be saved, Jesus' sacrifice would still have been enough if everyone had been saved.

What does that mean for the sins you've committed as a believer? Covered. His sacrifice is enough for your sin. All of your sin—past, present, future. "Where there is forgiveness of sins, there is no longer any offering for sin" (Heb. 10:18). No more punishment. No self-flagellation. No penance. No reason to live in shame.

14. Revelation 19:11.
15. Hebrews 7:25.

Our advocate, Jesus Christ the Righteous, knows what it's like to be us. We don't have a Savior who is distant or aloof or disconnected from the human experience. He knows what it is to be human, to be tempted, to feel the way we do. He sympathizes with our weaknesses.[16] He doesn't scowl, point fingers, or take back His propitiation. He tells us to run to Him so that when we are in need, we'll find the mercy and grace we need to stand firm and endure.[17] That's a promise you can hold on to when you can't remember who you are.

LEAVE THE CORPSE ALONE

Sometimes the noxious pull of temptation is overpowering. We forget that sin never satisfies, that disobedience is full of empty promises, that a moment of weakness can lead to days, weeks, even *years* of regret. Much of the time, when it comes to a face-off with sin, we forget that we're not as strong as we think we are.[18] And sometimes, we run straight for the momentary pleasure it gives. You can insert your vice here: pornography, gluttony, drunkenness, envy, pride, lust, anger, hatred. Whatever it is, you know the sound of its siren song, you know the tug to imbibe just this once, you weigh its fleeting pleasure against the muted call of obedience. And in a moment, you choose to forget that this—this pursuit, this action, this person who runs after empty vainglories—isn't who you are anymore.

When we run toward sin, we're forgetting that our old selves were executed.[19] We're purposefully forgetting so we can resurrect

---

16. Hebrews 4:15.
17. Hebrews 4:16.
18. I'm grateful for the late Rich Mullins for this line from his song "We Are Not As Strong As We Think We Are" (1996, Universal Music Publishing Group).
19. Galatians 2:20.

what's supposed to be dead. John Stott calls this purposeful for-getfulness "nail-drawing." It's going back to the cross where we crucified our flesh with Jesus, drawing out the nails, and trying to pull the corpse back down. He wrote:

> It is as if, having nailed our old nature to the cross, we keep wistfully returning to the scene of its execution. We begin to fondle it, to caress it, to long for its release, even to try to take it down again from the cross. *We need to learn to leave it there.* When some jealous, or proud, or malicious, or impure thought invades our mind we must kick it out at once. It is fatal to begin to examine it and consider whether we are going to give in to it or not. We have declared war on it; we are not going to resume negotiations. We have settled the issue for good; we are not going to re-open it. We have crucified the flesh; we are never going to draw the nails.[20]

This is who you are in Christ—you're new. "For you have died, and your life is hidden with Christ in God" (Col. 3:3). You've settled this at the cross. So don't run where you think the Lord can't find you. Your sin is never hidden from Him, and He desires for the old you to stay nailed to the cross. He has dressed you in robes of righteousness, and declared your debt forgiven. No more nail-pulling. Leave those old iterations of yourself nailed to the cross where Jesus made it possible for you to be known, loved, and free. Don't run toward the empty promises of the things that would have dragged your soul to hell had God not intervened and turned your heart toward His. Run to Him instead. Again and again and again.

---

20. John Stott, *The Message of Galatians: Only One Way* (InterVarsity, 1968), 151–52. (Emphasis mine.)

When you are weak, He is strong. When you've sinned, He has not. He gave you His obedience to wear like a robe, so wear it. And sin no more.

KNOWN AND UNASHAMED

"Where shall I go from your Spirit? Where shall I flee from your presence?" Psalm 139 beckons us to look at the fullness of God, the way He fills the earth with His glory, the way He inhabits the praises and the hearts of His people, the way He delighted in removing your reproach. He has not treated us as our sins deserve. Instead, He fixed our sin problem. He removed our shame and dressed us in the righteousness of His Son. Wherever you go, He is there. Whatever you try to hide, He has already seen. If your heart is His, there is no corner you can keep Him out of. He is too big and too good to leave those shadowed, shame-filled places alone. He elbows in, turning on lights and casting a beam on the places we think we can't be free from. He exposes our sin so that we will flee from it.

The Lord knows you. He has seen what's in your heart and how you've felt. He's seen when you've hidden and when you've run. He doesn't hold you at arm's length but always welcomes you back.

He is the father who looks for His wandering son and runs to meet him.

He is the shepherd who looks for the one errant sheep and brings her home.

He is the Savior who laid down His life to save you.

You do not have to live in shame over yesterday's sins or today's. Instead confess your sin and let the Lord forget it. Run to Him. Even when you sin. *Especially* when you sin. Leave the corpse alone and stay close to the One who stays close to you. You are never lost when you're held by the right hand of the One who made you new.

○   ○   ○

for further thought:

1. Do you feel shame for pre-conversion sins? Read 1 John 1:9. What do you learn about God's character that assures you your sins have been forgiven?

2. Do you feel shame for post-conversion sins? Read 1 John 2:1–6 again. What about Jesus' role as our advocate helps us to put off shame and walk in righteousness instead?

3. What do you learn about God's character from Psalm 139:7–10?

4. Why is practicing penance or self-flagellation antithetical to the gospel?

5. Read Colossians 3:1–17. When we feel tempted to return to old areas of sin and disobedience to God, what should we remember about our new identity in Christ?

Where shall I go from your Spirit?

Or where shall I flee from your presence?

If I ascend to heaven, you are there!

If I make my bed in Sheol, you are there!

If I take the wings of the morning

and dwell in the uttermost parts of the sea,

even there your hand shall lead me,

and your right hand shall hold me.

PSALM 139:11–12

If I say, "Surely the darkness shall cover me,

and the light about me be night,"

even the darkness is not dark to you;

the night is bright as the day,

for darkness is as light with you.

4

Known in the Dark

Does God See My Hidden Pain?

On April 8, 2024, the sky went dark in the middle of the day. It was only for a couple of minutes, but I'd never seen a total solar eclipse before, and I was not prepared for what I saw.

We knew about the eclipse, of course. Our little Missouri town was directly in the path of totality, so festivals and viewing parties were in the works *years* before the actual event. Having missed the 2017 eclipse because of only partial coverage, I didn't see what the big deal was or why everyone was so hyped up about something that lasts only three minutes. Nevertheless, my husband and I set up lawn chairs at a local park, and I laughed at all the cars with out-of-state license plates that filled up the parking lot. Why would you travel to another state for this?

We sat for an hour or so, glancing up at the sun with our eclipse glasses. Little by little, the moon crept across the face of the sun. The light was sepia-toned, like light that belonged in a dream where everything is just odd enough to let you know you're not really awake. Suddenly, the temperature dropped and everything quieted. I threw my eclipse glasses on the ground and gasped at the dark night sky. It was 1:57 p.m. Cheers erupted throughout the park as the silvery ring around the moon glimmered against a navy sky filled with stars. Red flares burst out from the lower left quadrant of the moon-covered sun. I twirled around to see the 360-degree sunset I'd heard about. Turning back to the night sky, I stared with all my might, begging my brain to hold on to the image. Too quickly it was over. The moon continued its path, the sky brightened, and the sun took over. I was surprised to find tears running down my cheeks.

THE CREATOR OF LIGHT AND DARK

I couldn't stop thinking about the eclipse for weeks after it happened. One thought pulsed in my mind as I stood in the park and watched the moon cover our source of light and heat: "What is man that you are mindful of him?"[1] How could the God who orchestrated such majesty take notice of humans who are usually less impressive than a total solar eclipse? I had the same thought when I stood on the edge of a cliff at Big Sur in northern California with my sister several years ago. Faced with the vastness of the Pacific, I couldn't grasp the One who spoke it into being. (For what it's worth, I cried on the edge of the cliff too.) I think that's what we ought to do with creation: gasp at its Maker. Wonder at who He is and how He could bend Himself so low as to care about our bodies and minds and spirits. But He does. He *does.*

"In the beginning, God created the heavens and the earth." The first sentence of the Bible tells us the first important thing for us to know about God. He was there before anything else existed and He's the one who made anything that exists. Genesis 1 goes on to tell us that "the earth was without form and void, and darkness was over the face of the deep. And the Spirit of

---

1. Psalm 8:4.

God was hovering over the face of the waters" (Gen. 1:2). There's a lot of mystery wrapped up in that verse, but essentially, it was dark when He created the universe. And then—"Let there be light," He said. "And there was light" (Gen. 1:3). We learn from Genesis 1 that God separated the light from darkness, calling the light Day and the dark Night. Evening and morning. Time divided. Time *invented*. In verses 14–19, God sets the stars and planets in their orbits, lighting up the sky and guiding the changing of the seasons with rotations and revolutions. God created light and dark, and He called it good.

What is true about God when the sun is up is true about Him when the sun has set.

It stands to reason, then, that when we get to Psalm 139:11–12, darkness isn't something that pushes God away, scares Him, fools Him, deters Him, or prevents Him from accomplishing His purposes. He is not threatened by the nighttime substance of time and shadow. He is not intimidated by His own creation. It all belongs to Him. "Yours is the day, yours also the night," the psalmist writes.[2] God created time itself and its divisions of light and dark, and that means there is nothing beneath the cover of darkness that escapes His notice.

But we're different, aren't we? Night takes on a threatening edge to us. The dark of night is when fear rears its ugly head, when anxieties multiply, when sleep eludes us because the stillness of the shadows gives us the opportunity to think. To remember. To feel. To hurt.

We often equate darkness with bad things—shame, regret, pain, sorrows, sin. But if God owns the night just like He owns the day, then what is true about Him when the sun is up is true

2. Psalm 74:16.

about Him when the sun has set. His character does not change, even when our fears and griefs are amplified under the cover of darkness. Whether it's a nighttime surge of pain and fear or a dark night of the soul when despair steals your joy, God remains the same. God remains true. God knows you in the dark.

HE SEES YOU IN THE DARK

Nights used to be really hard for me. I spent nearly fourteen years in crushing nightly pain due to an autoimmune disorder. My pain ramped up after an hour or two in bed, making it impossible to sleep. More than a decade of broken sleep led to increased brain fog, troubling anxiety, chronic insomnia, and the incessant worry that nothing would ever change. Everything in my life was worse at night. And as I've spoken to friends and family members with similar struggles, their anxieties and fears also loom much larger at night than they do during the day. We can speak logic into our fears when the sun is out; our anxieties seem to shrink when warmed with light. Turn out the lamp at night and try to sleep, though; those same sorrows and trials grow long shadows of hopelessness in the dark.

I've found my generation to be a bit more forthcoming about personal suffering than the previous one. Whether we're gathered with a prayer group, having coffee with a friend, or writing a post for social media, we're generally okay sharing personal details about our current struggles. Many in my parents' and grandparents' generations were a good deal more reserved, a trait I've found to be typical of those generations represented in my own church family. But regardless of how transparent we are with other people, there is a level of understanding that's missing unless someone has lived through the same trial you have. And even if someone has, there are still subtle differences, varied levels of spiritual maturity at the outset of the trial, all kinds of personality traits that make the trial a different experience for each person. Human beings are complicated like that. We long to be understood and truly known in our sorrows so that others can sympathize in a way that's not patronizing or nominal. But much of the time, we're misunderstood, our suffering is generalized, and we feel alone in the dark.

We might wonder if God even cares about our unseen, personal pain. If I walk the floors in pain all night and nobody sees, did it even happen? But God does see. God does know.

I spent many nights during those fourteen years pacing the floors in my house while my family slept. I tried reading, praying, journaling, reciting Scripture—anything to help quell the fear in my chest that bloomed as my physical pain increased. In the morning, though, I'd tiredly go through my routine and try to have as normal a day as anyone else. I looked completely healthy. My disease was hidden, internal, giving few visible clues to the level of agony I dealt with on a nightly basis. No one, not even my loyal husband, understood how deep the ache in my bones, how gripping the crucible of pain. I could try to explain it, but unless they'd felt the piercing pain of spondylitis themselves, my words failed to communicate the depth of my suffering. No one could truly understand. No one, that is, except the Lord. And that is the only truth that helped me persevere through those dark nights.

My suffering, so profoundly present in the dark, was not hidden from Him. And neither is yours. "He reveals deep and hidden things; he knows what is in the darkness, and the light dwells with him" (Dan. 2:22). We might keep our trials to ourselves because we are embarrassed to share them and leery of garnering undue attention. We might wonder if God even cares about our unseen, personal pain. If I walk the floors in pain all night and nobody sees, did it even happen? But that's the thing, God does see. God does know. And since His omniscience isn't passive, as we've discussed, His knowledge connotes care. His knowledge means investment. Maybe no one else sees, understands, or even knows about your personal suffering, but the God who split time into day and night sees, understands, and knows about it.

Jesus explained the Father's intimate care for us when He preached the Sermon on the Mount. "Look at the birds of the air; they neither sow nor reap nor gather into barns, and yet your heavenly Father feeds them. Are you not of more value than they?" (Matt. 6:26). And later, when talking about the suffering that comes to His followers for His name's sake, Jesus returns to God's personal concern for the suffering of His children: "So have no fear of them, for nothing is covered that will not be revealed, or hidden that will not be known. What I tell you in the dark, say in the light, and what you hear whispered, proclaim on the housetops. And do not fear those who kill the body but cannot kill the soul. Rather fear him who can destroy both soul and body in hell" (Matt. 10:26–28).

The unseen suffering that Christians endure for the name of Jesus is seen by the Father—known by Him. It matters to Him. Jesus returns to the sparrows to underscore His point: "Are not two sparrows sold for a penny? And not one of them will fall to the ground apart from your Father. But even the hairs of your head are numbered. Fear not, therefore; you are of more value than many sparrows" (Matt. 10:29–31).

It's springtime as I write this chapter, and we recently had a spate of storms move through with high winds and heavy rain. I left my house for an early morning walk after the weather pushed out of the area, and as I was setting the workout function on my watch, I nearly stepped on a tiny dead bird in our driveway. It was a sparrow, probably fallen from a nest in the large tree that hangs over my driveway. I thought about the fallen sparrow as I walked that morning. This little bird is one of how many that have lived through history? *How many birds?* Still, God knew its end date. It didn't die in the storm without His knowledge.

Your hidden suffering is seen by Him, for darkness is not dark to the Lord.

A few days ago, I lay in the basket swing in our backyard and watched a pair of mourning doves tucked up into a branch of the tulip tree. One dove poked and prodded the other until it flew away, looking a little peeved.

Our house is nearly a hundred years old and sits in a yard with equally aged and mature trees. It's a shady haven for all kinds of birds: sparrows, doves, robins, blue jays, cardinals, starlings, and those annoying mockingbirds that swoop at us when we get too close. While I'm not a "birder" and I have no intentions of becoming one in this mid-life season I'm in, it's good for me to stop and consider the birds, as Jesus instructed. God knows not only every genus and species, but He also determines the lifespan of every bird that has ever lived and died. He is (humor me, please) the ultimate birder. But as Jesus points out, if the Father is that invested in *birds*, how much more is He invested in *your* life? You matter more than birds! You are, as we'll learn in the next chapter, made in God's very image—a fact that separates you from birds in so many ways.

If the death of a bird is noticed by God, how much more the suffering of His children? Your hidden suffering is seen by Him, for as our psalmist demonstrates, darkness is not dark to the Lord. Night shines as "bright as the day" with Him.[3] Nothing is hidden from His sight, whether we're trying to hide it, or life circumstances make us feel invisible to the rest of the world.

But we forget about the birds, don't we? Suffering makes you feel alone and lonely. It leads you to question God, to wonder how long He'll allow you to walk through the valley of the shadow of death. But the promise of Scripture is that He not only knows about our suffering, He's with us in the midst of it.

HE IS WITH YOU IN THE DARK

Psalm 23 speaks to the faithfulness of God's presence in our suffering. "Even though I walk through the valley of the shadow of death, I will fear no evil, for you are with me; your rod and your staff, they comfort me" (Ps. 23: 4). He's not only aware of your dark suffering, He's the shepherd who guides you through it, protecting your heart as He walks you to the other side. You need not fear in the middle of the night when pain presses your body or fear suffocates your peace—He is with you. Present. True. Strong. The fear and pain you feel are neither fearful nor crushing to Him. Remember, He already knows what's hidden in the darkness, and light dwells with Him.[4] When you're unsure of God's love in the night, He is not threatened by those doubts. He is as real and strong and true as He has ever been. His presence in the shadowed valley is not diminished by your doubts, nor is it weakened by your fear.

3. Psalm 139:12.
4. Daniel 2:22.

The Lord may seem like a silent presence in the dark, but He is not idle. Scripture tells us that both the Spirit who lives in you and Jesus who is seated at the right hand of the Father are interceding for you. If you've ever wondered where Jesus is, He's sitting at the right hand of the Father praying for you. Let that sink in: Jesus is praying for you. And the Holy Spirit is praying for you. *You.* The author of Hebrews writes: "Consequently, he is able to save to the uttermost those who draw near to God through him, since he always lives to make intercession for them" (Heb. 7:25). When Jesus died on the cross for our sins, He bridged the gap between sinful man and holy God, making it possible for us to have a restored relationship with the Father as our sins were forgiven. Unlike the priests of the old covenant who never rested because they had to keep making sacrifices for the ongoing sin of man, Jesus was raised from the dead, ascended to heaven, and sat down at His Father's side because His work of atonement was perfect and complete. Finished. Done. And what is He doing in the meantime while we wait for His return? Praying for us. He "lives to make intercession" for us.

And if that wasn't enough, the Holy Spirit who indwells believers prays for us as well.

> Likewise the Spirit helps us in our weakness. For we do not know what to pray for as we ought, but the Spirit himself intercedes for us with groanings too deep for words. And he who searches hearts knows what is the mind of the Spirit, because the Spirit intercedes for the saints according to the will of God. (Rom. 8:26–27)

I've had nights of pain and anxiety and fear when I do not even know how to properly pray. I spin words that don't make sense, don't add up, and probably aren't even theologically right. This isn't problematic for the Lord because the Holy Spirit is praying in my place, making my prayers better. His prayers are perfect because He knows God's will and prays accordingly. He "prays those things we ought to pray."[5]

The key here—because Hebrews 7 and Romans 8 are in agreement—is to *draw near to God* in the dark because you have Jesus and the Spirit on your side, bringing you close to the Father with their perfect prayers. God is not ashamed of you in the dark. Whatever it is that plagues you—pain, regret, fear, anxiety, doubt—He sees it, the Spirit articulates it, Jesus prays for it, the Father knows it. You do not carry it alone.

HE DOES NOT DESPISE YOU IN THE DARK

Jesus died a humiliating death for us. Stripped naked, forced to carry His executionary implement, spat upon, falsely accused, propped up publicly as a spectacle to be sneered at and an example to recuse yourself from. Even His closest friends distanced themselves from Him in His darkest hour. Jesus, through whom God spoke light and darkness into existence,[6] suffered the reproach of the cross because of your sin and mine. He carried both our sorrows and our sins on His shoulders, bearing the weight of judgment that we deserve. He suffered a painful physical death in addition to the indefinable agony of making atonement for us. "My God, my God, why have you forsaken me?" Jesus cried out from the cross, echoing the psalmist in Psalm 22:1. But if you read all of Psalm 22, you learn that God did not despise His Son in His darkest agony: "For he has not

5. Megan Hill, *Praying Together: The Priority and Privilege of Prayer in Our Homes, Communities, and Churches* (Crossway, 2016), 24.
6. Colossians 1:16.

despised or abhorred the affliction of the afflicted, and he has not hidden his face from him, but has heard, when he cried to him" (Ps. 22:24).

I feel certain that Jesus, who is the Word of God Himself, knew the weight of those words at the cross. God did not despise His Son when He suffered in our place at the cross but rather *heard* His prayers. This should deeply encourage us in our own sufferings. Not only do we have an advocate in Jesus who understands what it's like to be us, dealing with temptation and rejection and physical suffering, but we also have a Father who does not despise those who are suffering. Rather, He hears our prayers and beckons us to draw near. He heard Jesus' prayers.[7] Because Jesus makes a way for us, God also hears our prayers.

Draw near, He tells us. It's this *drawing near* that we must do when we feel lost in the darkness of sorrow or shame or sin. That's where and when we're guaranteed to find mercy and grace when we need it most. "For we do not have a high priest who is unable to sympathize with our weaknesses, but one who in every respect has been tempted as we are, yet without sin" (Heb. 4:15). We have an advocate who understands. He doesn't draw back ashamed of our weaknesses. So neither should we draw back too embarrassed of our weaknesses. Rather we should run to Him. Run to the One who understands what it's like to be human and frail and fraught with weakness and weary of temptation. He conquered all of it so that we can therefore "with confidence draw near to the throne of grace, that we may receive mercy and find grace to help in time of need" (Heb. 4:16).

Did you catch that? It's a promise. When you draw near to God—with all your weaknesses, fear, doubt, pain, and sorrow—

---

7. Hebrews 5:7

you will receive mercy and find grace when you need it most. You *will* receive mercy; you *will* find grace. Why? Because Jesus knows what it's like to be weak. And rather than pull away from us when we're broken and undesirable, He gives us what we need most to endure: mercy, grace. "He cannot bear to leave us alone to fend for ourselves."[8]

Why then would we pull away from Him in the night? Why would we turn elsewhere for comfort when He is our very means of survival? There's no need to hide your pain from Him. He sees you. He knows you. He's praying for you. Won't *His* prayers be rightly answered?

KNOWN AND SEEN

What is it that keeps you up at night? What do you fear when the lights go out and all is quiet but the turmoil rising in your soul? The shame, fear, or pain that clench tightly around your body or heart are no match for the Lord. Dark is not dark to Him. He is the light of the world, and all our troubles in this life will one day wither beneath the beams of His certain victory.

There's nothing in your life—no form of suffering, no entanglement with sin—that's too much or too embarrassing for you to bring into the light before God. No matter your physical or spiritual age, your calling as a believer in Jesus is to walk humbly with Him. That means letting Him shine a light on the things we want to keep hidden from others. Hidden things lose their power when brought into the light of Christ. But you'll have to swallow your embarrassment, remembering that Jesus knows what it's like to be human, and ask for His help.

8. Dane Ortlund, *Gently and Lowly: The Heart of Christ for Sinners and Sufferers* (Crossway, 2020), 91.

In Mark 5, a woman with a gynecological bleeding disorder approached Jesus for healing. She'd been dealing with the bleeding for twelve years, and her illness had impoverished her and rendered her ceremonially unclean for much of her life.[9] An illness like this would likely have caused infertility and public shame. I've dealt with infertility and incredibly painful gynecological disorders for decades. Though I live in an age and culture when infertility and female issues don't carry nearly the same shameful stigma they did when she lived, I've still experienced the helplessness a diagnosis like this delivers. You can exhaust your financial resources chasing medical help, but in the end—with a case like hers and mine—there's little you can do to change your circumstances. You can only draw near to God with faith that He might change *you*.

Destitute and desperate, this poor but determined woman worked her way through the crowds that thronged Jesus, believing that if she touched just the hem of Jesus' robe, she could be made well. Touching a person while still dealing with a bleeding disorder would have rendered them also ceremonially unclean, but when she touched Jesus, His purity and power overwhelmed that uncleanness and made her well. He was greater than her ongoing sorrow, her physical suffering, and her public shame. What she had suffered in the dark, He overcame in the light. He wasn't ashamed of her. Rather, He healed her and commended her faith.

This woman shows us what it looks like to swallow your pride, suffer the risk of embarrassment, and draw near to the only One who offers lasting hope. She could have continued suffering in isolation. But in faith she let what was hidden come

9. Leviticus 15:19–30.

to light, for Scripture tells us that Jesus was perfectly aware of all that happened in that moment when she reached for the hem of His robe.[10]

That's all we're doing when we draw near, really. We're reaching for the hem of His robe, groping in the dark for the One who is stronger and surer than us. We're drawing near in faith, knowing that Jesus is aware of our suffering and praying for us in it. He doesn't just see us. He's with us. He isn't just with us, He's praying for us. He isn't just praying for us, He's giving us exactly what we need in the dark night of the body and soul. He's giving us mercy and grace in Himself.

This is what it means to be known in the dark, friend. Reach for the hem of His robe. You'll find mercy and grace.

○ ○ ○

for further thought:

1. Why do you think our problems seem worse at night?

2. What are you suffering from or struggling with that keeps you up at night? Do you feel unseen and/or misunderstood in this area?

3. David says that "even the darkness is not dark to you" in Psalm 139:12. What do you learn, both literally and figuratively, about God's character?

4. Read Hebrews 4:14–16, Hebrews 7:25, and Romans 8:26–30. What do the Father, Son, and Holy Spirit do for

10. Mark 5:30.

us to help us endure? Describe their investment in your perseverance in suffering or fighting sin.

5. Why should the story of the woman in Mark 5 encourage us to draw near to the Lord in our suffering? What do you learn about Jesus from that story?

For you formed my inward parts;
    you knitted me together in my mother's womb.
I praise you, for I am fearfully and wonderfully
    made.
Wonderful are your works;
    my soul knows it very well.
My frame was not hidden from you,
when I was being made in secret,
    intricately woven in the depths of the earth.
Your eyes saw my unformed substance;
in your book were written, every one of them,
    the days that were formed for me,
    when as yet there was none of them.

How precious to me are your thoughts, O God!
    How vast is the sum of them!
If I would count them, they are more than the
    sand.
    I awake, and I am still with you.

5

Known in
Body and Soul

Why Is My Body Like This?

I read a novel recently that bothered me from the very first page. I could tell from the first few paragraphs that I was dealing with what literature calls an *unreliable narrator*. Written in first person, the protagonist told the story in a way that made him the hero when the last chapter revealed that he was, in fact, the antagonist. *He* was the sociopath, the liar, the one leaving out important details of the story that would have incriminated him early on. I could tell whatever story he was weaving would have large holes, purposefully dropped stitches that would tangle the plot and the setting. I could tell he was using this yarn of his to hang the supporting characters and their credibility.

I'll be honest: I hated that book. You can't trust an unreliable narrator to tell you the truth about anything, least of all himself.

THE UNRELIABLE NARRATORS

I have a friend from church who faithfully remembers everyone's birthday. Without fail, her birthday card or social media birthday post will include a cheerful reminder from Psalm 139:14. She always writes: "You are fearfully and wonderfully made!" I love that about my friend Wendy. She is, in a small but thoughtful way, pushing back against the stories we tell ourselves about our bodies, our lives, our minds, our very selves. She is telling the truth about each person she knows—they were created by God in His image and their life matters to Him.

I remember the first time I hated my body. I was at a friend's house, laughing and talking, lazing away a long summer day back before social media, streaming television, or smartphones existed. We were trying on each other's clothes the way girls do, ever on a hunt for something new to wear. But my friend's long lean jeans didn't fit my body. I was short for my age (still am) and had never really compared my body with someone else's before. Where she was willowy and spread out, I was petite and compact. "They won't fit you," she told me. "You're husky, you know." I left her house bewildered. Husky? *My body is bad*, I remember thinking. *My body is wrong*. Barely weighing sixty pounds soaking wet, my opinion of my body was forever changed. I was nine years old.

My disdain of my physical form blossomed with my body during puberty. In high school, I compared my pants size to every girl I knew. Smaller was better. It was the 1990s, and fat was the enemy of every female. I tried every diet I heard about: the low-fat diet, the vegetarian diet, the cabbage soup diet (I still shudder at that one), the Slim-Fast diet,[1] the Special K diet,[2] and finally—the starve-all-day-and-try-not-to-faint-during-school diet. That was

---

1. A 1990s low-calorie meal replacement drink that was as disappointing in taste as it was in nutrition.
2. I can't imagine why anyone thought replacing two meals a day with low-calorie cereal would be good for our nutrition.

the one I clung to the longest, punishing my body while it tried to grow as designed. I was always hungry.

The unreliable narrator of my childhood and teen years told me a damaging story about myself that was colored by our culture's unattainable standards of beauty. I struggled with various forms of disordered eating for years because of the one comment from a ten-year-old that I chose to believe with all my heart, soul, mind, and strength. Believing that one opinion about my body led me to weave a narrative about myself that shaped my heart and mind for decades. My mind was the protagonist; my body was the antagonist. But because I was an embodied soul, I was both hero and villain, locked in a war I was destined to lose.

That unreliable narrative didn't end when I became an adult.

While I eat and work out for my health these days, I must be on guard when it comes to the story I believe about my body. I must fence my mind with truth about the physical shell God has given me. And these days, the narrative isn't merely about weight or beauty. I was diagnosed with primary infertility when I was twenty-four, and nothing made me feel more betrayed than a body that wouldn't do what it was designed to do. Every woman I knew was able to get pregnant and give birth. But not me. *This body is bad. This body is wrong.* This body is the villain.

When I was almost thirty, a prolonged season of extreme stress began to affect my physical health. Long bouts of grief and insomnia seemed to trigger an unknown illness into activity. Six years later, I was finally diagnosed with a cluster of autoimmune diseases. If you're unfamiliar with autoimmune diseases, they often begin displaying symptoms after a significant hormonal shift (e.g., pregnancy or childbirth) or a stressful or traumatic event.[3] Several years into my mysterious but crippling symptoms of chronic pain, digestive problems, brain fog, numerous vitamin and mineral deficiencies, and rashes, I developed anxiety as well. I was locked in a cycle of physical pain and mental distress. *This body is bad. This body is wrong.* Again, my body was the villain I could not seem to conquer or control.

I've lived with infertility for twenty years now and my diseases nearly as long, and much of the time, I struggle to believe anything good about my body. I am the unreliable narrator in this story, and I find it very hard to believe that my body is fearfully *or* wonderfully made.

While it's likely that female readers will find much in common with my narrative about my body, I'm sure there are male readers who struggle with their appearance, their health, or the way their bodies seem to have failed them as well. This isn't just a female issue. Neither is it always a visible issue. You might fight depression or bipolar disorder, feeling uncertain about the stability of your mind, You might wish you were like everyone else, that your brain didn't have so many plot holes or self-sabotaging chapters. Your unreliable narrator tells you: *Your body is bad. Your body is wrong.*

Whatever the struggle with your human frame, we all seem to be very willing to believe the unreliable narrators about the value

3. The research on autoimmune diseases is still woefully lacking, but studies seem to be making a connection between trauma or persistent stress and the eventual diagnosis of disease. Having lived with multiple autoimmune diseases for nearly two decades, I can trace the awakening of my diseases to a prolonged season of immense personal anguish. Additionally, flareups seem to coincide with significant episodes of stress, which have an inflammatory effect on the body. This study from Harvard at least entertains the connection, though far more research would be helpful in identifying root causes and subsequent treatments: Robert H. Shmerling, MD, "Autoimmune Disease and Stress: Is There a Link?" Harvard Health Publishing, October 27, 2020, https://www.health.harvard.edu/blog/autoimmune-disease-and-stress-is-there-a-link-2018071114230.

of our bodies. We are, however, reluctant to believe what God has said about the bodies He Himself created.

THE RELIABLE NARRATOR

Psalm 139 is often heralded for its high view of human life. For anyone firmly committed to celebrate the dignity of life from womb to tomb, these four verses underscore the inherent value of personhood—before a person is even born.

> For you formed my inward parts; you knitted me together in my mother's womb. I praise you, for I am fearfully and wonderfully made. Wonderful are your works; my soul knows it very well. My frame was not hidden from you, when I was being made in secret, intricately woven in the depths of the earth. Your eyes saw my unformed substance; in your book were written, every one of them, the days that were formed for me, when as yet there were none of them. (Ps. 139:13–16)

What makes a life valuable? David tells us in verses 13–16. *God* makes a life valuable. Being created by God imbues our lives with meaning and value and purpose. Notice the action verbs in the above verses: formed, knitted, made, woven, saw, written. God is the one creating, and this is what He did to bring you into existence: He formed you—every cell. He knitted you together in your mother's womb, quietly growing you where no one could see. He put you together and His tools were awe and wonder. He saw you when no one else could. He wrote your story from beginning to end, from first word to last, before you were *you*. Your days were written in His book long before you became a person with a story. Before sperm met egg

What makes a life valuable? God makes a life valuable.

and began the process of cell division, God knew you. Loved you. Imbued your first moment of existence in the depths of your mother's womb with *meaning*.

God is the reliable narrator who made you with care and love. He was both purposeful and creative in making you. Even knowing that the package He'd wrap your soul in would be harmed by sin's reach, He still chose to make you in His image. And His work was very good.

HIS WORK IS VERY GOOD

When God created Adam and Eve, it was different than His creative work to that point. Light and dark, day and night, planets and stars—what wonderous displays of His creative handiwork! You've already heard me blather on about the moon passing in front of the sun and how I almost didn't recover from the 2024 total solar eclipse. And that's just *one* celestial event. Yet when you look at Genesis 1, you'll see that the stars and sky and planets and galaxies were deemed *good* in God's estimation.[4] Heavenly bodies we've only recently glimpsed through the James Webb Telescope stop our hearts with wonder and a little fear. But God calls the matter that makes up those glimpses *good*.

Next, God made trees and forests and plants and rivers and mountains. He looked around with pleasure. Still *good*. I stood on the edge of a cliff at Big Sur again recently and felt my insignificance down to my bones. Yet God calls the breath-catching wonder of that Pacific coastline *good*. I look up and up and up at the hundred-year-old trees in my yard and God called the trees *good*.

4. Genesis 1:18.

But then comes God's creation of man and woman, and something here is so different, so wildly, attention-grabbingly different. Unlike every other aspect of His expansive creation, man and woman are made in the image of the Creator Himself. "So God created man in his own image, in the image of God he created him; male and female he created them" (Gen. 1:27). God puts them in charge of the created order on earth, looks out over what He's made, and calls it "*very* good."[5]

How can a *person* be more impressive than the cliffs that have stood silent and strong to catch the pounding of the Pacific for millennia? How can a *person* hold more wonder than the Swiss Alps or a total eclipse? Here it is: Nothing else in the universe bears the image of its Maker. Only humans. In a sermon on Psalm 8, Tim Keller explained what it means to be made in the image of God. He said that *imago Dei* means we have a rational aspect, a personal aspect, an eternal aspect, and a creative aspect—all of which set us apart from the rest of creation.[6]

> God made human beings so high and noble that we are just short of divinity. . . . We have got things that only God has. . . . In all these things we're just a little lower than the [angels], or just short of divinity. We're below the divinity but above all the rest of the created order. In other words, God has made us crowned with His own glory and honor.[7]

Out of all the things He made, God created us to be lower than Him but most like Him. This was intentional. This was

---

5. Genesis 1:31.

6. Timothy Keller, "The Search for Identity" on Psalm 8, of the series "Modern Problems, Ancient Solutions" preached at Redeemer Presbyterian Church on October 10, 1993, https://podcast.gospelinlife.com/e/the-search-for-identity/.

7. Keller, "The Search for Identity."

something He exulted in. As Psalm 8 tells us, God has "crowned [us] with glory and honor"—His own glory and honor that He gives us through Jesus. God delighted in doing this. He chose to do this. And He did it as my friend Wendy likes to remind everyone, fearfully and wonderfully. With awe and wonder. *Very good.*

I wonder sometimes why we are so willing to believe what anyone and everyone else says about our bodies rather than the One who made them. His opinion matters most, but it's His opinion we believe the least. It's like the times my husband cups my cheek with his hand and tells me I'm beautiful, and I make a cringey face and say "whatever" before pointing out my latest, most annoying flaw. In terms of human attractiveness, my husband's opinion of me matters most, but for some backward reason, it's his words I believe the least. Or *value* the least.

Something went wrong here.

WHERE DID OUR BODIES GO WRONG?

"It's the fall! It's sin!" you're thinking, and rightly so. God did create us "very good," but everything went very wrong when Adam and Eve sinned. We bear in our bodies the curse of sin and death. We are aging from the moment we take our first breath. We fight the coming of the end as soon as we begin to see its subtle pursuit in gray hair at our temples and crow's feet around our eyes. We feel its imminence when our joints ache in the morning and our energy wanes in the afternoon. And then there are those who are born with—or who eventually develop—maladies that cover the spectrum from mild to off-the-charts severe. Death is chasing us. Our bodies cry out that we are not as we were meant to be.

I sat in my rheumatologist's office for over an hour last fall detailing my health history for the past forty years. When we got to the end of it, tears streamed down my cheeks because all I could think was how much my body had failed me. "That's a *lot*," my doctor told me compassionately. I have often wanted to climb out of the physical frame that so poorly holds me together.

One day, I will.

My friend Whitney wrote in her book on death and grief, "Our bodies are wonderfully made in the image of God. Our bodies are terribly broken because of the fall. Both can be true."[8] She goes on to describe our frail flesh as we are meant to see it in light of the finished work of Christ at the cross.

> What if our longings for these bodies to do more, be more, and last longer are reminders that they were indeed made for more? In this light, the fading and frailty of our flesh is not pointless cruelty. Every wrinkle, every limp, every cancer cell can be both the result of sin *and* a gracious reminder. We can take heart, then, not because our bodies are ultimate, but because ultimately, they are signposts to somewhere.[9]

This body of mine has *gone* wrong but it is not altogether bad. God created me knowing things would go poorly when I was young. He knew I'd fight the pull of vanity as much as the havoc of disease. Even so, He knitted me together with care and kind intention. Because He created this body to die. And to live again

---

8. Whitney K. Pipkin, *We Shall All Be Changed: How Facing Death with Loved Ones Transforms Us* (Moody Publishers, 2024), 91.
9. Pipkin, *We Shall All Be Changed*, 91.

in its ultimate, best form. Sam Allberry has written that Christians have been raised spiritually, but not yet physically. "We're running new-creation software on old-creation hardware."[10]

THESE BODIES NEED A RESURRECTION

A few years ago, one of my closest friends passed away. Sue had fought GVHD, graft-versus-host disease, after a bone marrow transplant to treat leukemia. Her body could not handle the cancer, the eviscerated immune system, or the cells that just couldn't pretend to be hers. She'd been in the hospital for months, and because of the pandemic, isolated much of the time. Her husband, Gary, FaceTimed me as Sue's breaths began to weaken. Propping up the phone so I could see Sue's face, Gary let me say everything that was in my heart before her body failed for the last time. I choked on my words, every sentiment soaked in tears. Her skin was graying quickly. I'd witnessed the pressing of death before and knew her time was nearly up. She died shortly after I hung up the phone. "Go to Jesus," were my last words to my friend.

Sue is buried on a hill facing the sunrise. I have sat at her grave many times with a cup of coffee and an ache for her presence so fierce I can't breathe. She would have approved of the coffee but would have worried at my tears. "The last enemy to be destroyed is death, Sue," I've often told her in the cemetery.[11]

I read Tim Challies' book on grief after Sue died, and near the end, Tim tells of a dream he had after his son Nick suddenly

---

10. This quote has been attributed to Sam Allberry, though I was unable to find the original source. For a helpful and deeper treatise on the human body and God's design for it, I recommend his book *What God Has to Say About Our Bodies: How the Gospel Is Good News for Our Physical Selves* (Crossway, 2021).

11. 1 Corinthians 15:26.

passed away. In his dream, Tim runs through the cemetery telling everyone to wake up because it is Resurrection Day.

> Up and down the rows of graves I begin to run, shouting out glad tidings. "It's time! It's time!" I cry out. "It's time to rise!" I run up one row and down the next, my feet pounding over the uneven turf. . . . On the edge of that path of grass that has been tended by my hand and watered by my tears, I drop to my knees. In a tone that is confident and unwavering, I say, "It's time, my boy! It's time! Just one more minute and we'll hear the cry of command. . . . It's time to wake up! It's time to rise!"[12]

I picture Sue's spot on the hill. I see the ground cracking open. I see her body rising, for Paul said she would.[13] But it's different. It's her and it's not. It's her resurrected body, changed, new, the same, different, recognizable, unrecognizable. I think about Jesus after the disciples saw His empty tomb. He's unrecognizable. He's also recognizable. It's His body as the disciples remembered Him. It's His body with scars. Paul said that Jesus will "transform our lowly body to be like his glorious body" and that "we shall all be changed."[14] It's not we shall all be

David knew that God's work in creating him body and soul was very good. And so do you. You feel it when sleep washes over your body in the best way possible, when you've worked hard and are ready for rest.

---

12. Tim Challies, *Seasons of Sorrow: The Pain of Loss and the Comfort of God* (Zondervan Reflective, 2022), 179–80.
13. 1 Thessalonians 4:16.
14. Philippians 3:21; 1 Corinthians 15:51.

destroyed. It's changed. A resurrection is a change that still makes us *us*. Just better. Impenetrable. Indestructible. Eternal.

When Jesus returns for those who belong to Him, those who have already died in faith will be raised up. He will knit them back together with awe and wonder but this time without the curse of sin and death waiting in the wings to tear at the seams. This is what we are waiting for—to be caught up with Christ in our resurrected bodies to spend eternity with Him in His kingdom. We won't be ethereal spirits floating around untethered. Jesus had a body when He was raised. And so will we. Because bodies aren't bad. Bodies aren't wrong. Bodies house souls, and that is very good.

David understood the value of personhood wrapped in flesh. He praised God for His very good work: "Wonderful are your works; my soul knows it very well" (Ps. 139:14). Somewhere down deep in his bones, David knew that God's work in creating him body and soul was very good. And so do you. You see it when your skin heals over a cut or a scrape, cells reforming to make new skin. You feel it when sleep washes over your body in the best way possible, when you've worked hard and are ready for rest. You witnessed it when your baby was born or when your mother passed away—the way the body can enter the world and leave it.

You know that God's work in making you is very good when your hands hold your Bible and your eyes read the words, when your mind stills itself in prayer, when your arms wrap around another Christian in unity. It's evident in the way your heart has learned compassion and forgiveness, it's in your grip on a knife when you slice bread or make a salad for dinner. It's obvious when you look up and up and up at the stars on a dark clear night, the same stars God showed to Abraham so long ago because He knew you would be one of those stars, one of Abraham's descendants.[15] It's in the beating of your heart as you try to count the stars, if you can. God calls them by name. He calls you by name, too. The stars declare His glory. You declare His image.

Yes, His work in making you is wonderful. Very good work. He made you *you* because He delighted in making you in His image. Your life matters to Him. You are like the moon reflecting the light of the sun, radiating the image of the Father to those around you. Don't say it doesn't matter how you look or how you feel or what has gone wrong in your body. It *does* matter. You were made to image God and in the righteousness of Christ, you do. Can you say with David that God's work in making you is good? Does your soul know it well?

THOSE PURPOSEFUL IMPERFECTIONS

Even the things about your body that disappoint you can be purposeful, for they are preparing you for eternity. Paul encourages us: "So we do not lose heart. Though our outer self is wasting away, our inner self is being renewed day by day. For this light and momentary affliction is preparing for us an eternal weight of glory beyond all comparison, as we look not to the things that are seen but to the things that are unseen" (2 Cor. 4:16–18a).

Your outer self is wasting away—and you know it. The gray hair, the sagging skin, the excess weight you can't lose, the anxiety, the cancer, the arthritis, the chronic pain, the infertility, the heart disease. You know about the wasting away part. But, in the fading of your frame, God is doing work on your soul. As you live and suffer and barrel toward death, He is drawing you near, teaching

15. Genesis 15:5–6.

you to depend on His promise to make you new. He is sanctifying you, tipping your chin to look at Him rather than your insufficiencies. He is teaching you that nothing temporary here will last and also that everything here that matters will last forever. He is making you into His best version of you—the one that looks most like Jesus. Jesus, the exact imprint of the nature of God.[16]

One day you will fully image God without the darkness of sin or disease or pain or sorrow to diminish the picture. You won't fight the demons of eating disorders or depression in your resurrected form. You won't walk the floors at night with a body on fire or a mind in torment. You'll rise from the grave like Sue. Like Tim's son, Nick. Like my grandparents. Like my friend Debbie who died last spring in a house fire. Like the mother you miss. Like the babies you buried. Like Jesus. We'll rise. And our bodies will be changed. And it will be very, very good. Because God will resurrect something that was already good, and He will make it better. He will make it *best*.

His works are wonderful. Our souls know it well. We're "not suffering from anything that a good resurrection can't fix."[17]

KNOWN AND VALUED

Your life has inherent value because God made you in His image. Every human life has inherent value because every human life was made in the image of God. If you are in Christ, though, your life will go on imaging God forever and ever. He gives your life value. He gives your life meaning. His careful knitting and forming and shaping means something for you as a person. His

---

16. Hebrews 1:3.
17. Don Carson, quoting his friend Frank, "How Can a Good God Allow Suffering?: A Biblical Perspective," The Gospel Coalition, August 18, 2023, https://www.thegospelcoalition.org/sermon/how-can-a-good-god-allow-suffering/.

pen was full of purpose when He wrote the story of your life and put it in His book.

Listen to the reliable narrator. He is the Author of life itself. And He said that your life is hidden in Him. He has made you His own. This is *very good*.

○ ○ ○

for further thought:

1. What do you learn about God's character from Psalm 139:13–16?

2. What imbues a human life with meaning? What does that mean for every human, born and unborn? What does that mean for those with disabilities, dementia, or debilitating diseases?

3. Do you have trouble praising God for the way your body is made? Do you feel that God made a mistake in how He made you? Why or why not? How can you combat this with biblical truth?

4. Read 2 Corinthians 4:16–18. We will age no matter how vigilantly we pursue health or anti-aging practices. We can't outrun death. How can we view the internal work God is doing in us as we grow older and weaker?

5. Describe what you think our resurrection bodies will be like. What do you look forward to in your new resurrected body? How can you be thankful for the body God has given you now while you wait for that day?

For you formed my inward parts;

you knitted me together in my mother's womb.

I praise you, for I am fearfully and wonderfully

made.

Wonderful are your works;

my soul knows it very well.

My frame was not hidden from you,

when I was being made in secret,

intricately woven in the depths of the earth.

Your eyes saw my unformed substance;

in your book were written, every one of them,

the days that were formed for me,

when as yet there was none of them.

**PSALM
139:17–18**

How precious to me are your thoughts, O God!

How vast is the sum of them!

If I would count them, they are more than the

sand.

I awake, and I am still with you.

6

Known Among Many

Will Anyone Remember Me?

Speaking of cemeteries, have you walked through one recently?[1] I know it seems morbid, but whenever I attend a funeral with a graveside service, I always take a moment to note the grave markers as I walk through. The names, the ages, the family connections, the phrases used to describe the deceased—they tell us a short story. A haiku of a human soul. The dash between the birth and death dates represents a whole life lived. A whole life spent on this earth with hopes and dreams and work and sorrows and favorite desserts and annoying quirks and besetting sins and hidden talents. A whole life of love or longing for it, of joy or searching for it. Of illness or heartbreak, of hope or the hope of hope. It's all reduced to a dash on a stone in a garden of mostly forgotten ghosts.

A stroll through a cemetery will teach you to number your days.[2] That dash seems long while you're in it but achingly short when it ends. I see all those dates and dashes and wonder if

---

1. You can picture Sue's grave on the hill overlooking the park, if you need a visual here. There's a pond in the distance, and a playground with a pavilion just over a short rise. Her friend Jan is buried close by.
2. Psalm 90:12.

there's enough time to really leave my imprint on this earth. I don't want to be forgotten. I don't want to one day be only a dash. I want to be thought of, to be remembered.

To be remembered will mean I was known. And if I was known, perhaps I was loved.

TO BE NOTICED AND TO MATTER

One of the hallmarks of image bearers is the desire for one's life to matter. You don't see this with animals; it is a decidedly human trait. Take a quick scroll through your favorite social media app and you'll see profile after profile of people who want to be remembered, who seek to be unique, to make a mark on this world, to be noticed, to stand out. Even if they're remembered for something silly or quirky, it's better than the alternative. To be forgotten would be too great a disappointment to bear.

Though God made us with unique traits and appearances, we usually seek individualistic notoriety to stand out from the crowd of humanity. Think through your family tree or consider the lives of your closest friends. Do you see a longing for uniqueness or remembrance? Do you see the God-given desire to make a life count written in the stories of your loved ones?

My maternal grandfather was one of the first chiropractors to ever set up practice in the city of Memphis, Tennessee. My paternal grandmother kept what is now a valuable scrapbook of newspaper clippings and photos during World War II to help her process the war as a teenager. My dad has perfect pitch and can play any instrument he picks up. My mother has worked at her local pregnancy care center for over thirty years, offering hope and help to all kinds of women in crisis. My sister is a talented photographer with a unique eye for beauty. My brother has had a successful career in energy efficiency without ever going to college. In my family heritage is a desire to achieve, work, serve, and create. That, I believe, is God-given.

This innate desire to be special or memorable is God's design. He has set eternity in our hearts so we'll understand that little in this life will last forever.[3] So in true human form, we take that God-given desire, and we distort it. Though we bear God's image, we scramble for more. We thirst to *matter*. We work hard to make people love us. We build barns and then bigger barns to contain what we think will make this life worth living. We work to make sure those tombstone dashes represent a life well-lived, a life brimming with every conceivable joy, a life that is remembered and special.

In the end, though, are we chasing after the wind? Won't we all be reduced to dashes remembered by no one? Won't there come a day when someone strolls through a cemetery and wonders at the dash on your grave? Isn't there an immense possibility they'll pass you by because no one remembers your name anymore?

One of the things I love about writing books is knowing I'm leaving behind a body of work that will (Lord willing) outlive me. From childhood, I wanted to leave a mark on this world in some way, to make a kind of dent in history that proves my life mattered. As an adult, I write books that I hope will teach people about God. I write songs for my church to sing. I teach my kids about Jesus so they'll carry on the gospel heritage that was passed on to me. I disciple teenage girls so they'll still love the Lord when they're my age, the way church mentors did for me. I won't stop working to make my life matter. Like my family members, it's *in* me to prove my worth.

---

3. Ecclesiastes 3:11.

My family is not unique in our desire to live full, notable lives. We all work hard in our jobs, churches, and communities to make a noticeable difference. We raise our children to know and love Jesus, making sure the generation behind us is equipped to teach the gospel to the generation after them. We cultivate hobbies that express our creativity, create homes that reflect our personalities, and join causes that communicate our convictions.

That urge to matter is nearly primal. We want people to notice our endeavors, but what should matter more is that God notices. We want people to see our service, but it matters more that God sees. We want people to know we lived and loved and worked. But what is more important is that God knows about every moment contained within that gravestone dash. And it matters to *Him*.

GOD THINKS OF HIS PEOPLE WITH PLEASURE

We've spent sixteen verses from Psalm 139 working through God's knowledge of His people and the love that extends from that intimate care. We've looked at His presence, examined His creativity in our physical and spiritual forms. We've uncovered untruths about shame and sin and rejoiced in how the gospel expresses the way God feels about us. As the psalmist extols God's wonderful work in creating us in His image and ordering our days, he moves on to praise God for the vast extent of His thoughts. "How precious to me are your thoughts, O God!" he exclaims. "How vast is the sum of them!" It's been noted that during the waking hours, humans have about 6,000 thoughts.[4] There is no formula that can determine the number of thoughts the sovereign Creator of the universe has each day. So when the psalmist says, "How vast is the

4. Crystal Raypole, "How Many Thoughts Do You Have Each Day? And Other Things to Think About," *Healthline*, February 28, 2022, https://www.healthline.com/health/how-many-thoughts-per-day.

sum of them!" he really means *vast*. It's unknowable for us.

To reiterate his point, he goes on in verse 18: "If I would count them, they are more than the sand. I awake, and I am still with you." If he tried to count the number of thoughts God has, he would fall asleep as though he were counting grains of sand. And if he fell asleep and then awoke, he would find that God was faithfully present and keeping watch while he slept. These verses proclaim the otherness of God. Unlike humans, He does not need sleep. His thought processes and ways are higher and better than ours. When Paul asks, "For who has known the mind of the Lord?" it's a rhetorical question—no one has known more about God than what has been revealed to us through Scripture.[5] And while He has given us all we need to know in this life, He hasn't told us everything about Himself.[6] We can't know every thought of God—there are too many to count.

> *God not only notices His people but thinks of them. And not only thinks of them but takes pleasure in them.*

Notice, though, that the psalmist *rejoices* in the vastness of God's mind. This isn't a cause for fear. God knows everything and yet this is a reason to praise Him, not a reason to hide in fear and shame. The psalmist comfortably falls asleep thinking about God's many thoughts and wakes up to find Him just as faithful as He has always been. Keeping watch. Steady on. There's a sense of well-being in these words.[7]

---

5. Romans 11:34.

6. Similarly, John closes his gospel saying that no book could contain all the works that Jesus did (see John 21:25). I believe we'll spend eternity learning more and more about the Lord as we dwell with Him forever.

7. See also Psalm 4:8: "In peace I will both lie down and sleep; for you alone, O LORD, make me dwell in safety."

In the psalms, we find numerous pleas to be remembered, for the Lord to turn His face to them, for Him to remember His covenant, act on their behalf, and show them favor in their dire circumstances. The assumption from authors—through the inspiration of the Holy Spirit—is that God not only notices His people but thinks of them. And not only thinks of them but takes *pleasure* in them. Take these for example:

> "For the LORD hears the needy and does not despise his own people who are prisoners." (Ps. 69:33)

> "For you bless the righteous, O LORD; you cover him with favor as with a shield." (Ps. 5:12)

> "The LORD takes pleasure in those who fear him, in those who hope in his steadfast love." (Ps. 147:11)

> "The LORD takes pleasure in His people; he adorns the humble with salvation." (Ps. 149:4)

You may have noticed something here. God does takes pleasure in His people, but there are caveats attached: righteousness, fear, hope, humility. God blesses those who are righteous, lowly, reverent, and humble. While I might see glimmers of those traits in my life, they radiate dimly from a heart that is often selfish and prideful. You likely feel the same way. So what hope do we have that *any* of God's thoughts toward us are favorable? How can He take pleasure in someone He knows so well?

LOVE IS NOT HARD FOR GOD

One of our more problematic approaches to God's character is the unconscious assumption that God is bad at loving us. We separate His steadfast love from His righteous wrath and assume He can't love us because we're sinful. But He is perfectly able to execute justice without minimizing His love. His capacity to perfectly exhibit all of His traits without compromising one of them is part of what makes Him who He is. So, He can despise our *sin* without holding *us* at arm's length. He could save us without grumpiness. In fact, He could save us and be happy He did so.

John Piper points out God's pleasure to not only save us but to give us everything He has for us—indeed, His entire kingdom.

> [Jesus'] aim is to defeat the fear that God is not the kind of God who really wants to be good to us—that he is not really generous and helpful and kind and tender, but is basically irked with us—ill-disposed and angry. Sometimes, even if we believe in our heads that God is good to us, we may feel in our hearts that his goodness is somehow forced or constrained, perhaps like a judge who has been maneuvered by a clever attorney into a corner on some technicality of court proceeding, so he has to dismiss the charges against the prisoner whom he really would rather send to jail. But Jesus is at pains to help us not feel that way about God. He is striving in this verse to describe for us the indescribable worth and excellency of God's soul by showing the unbridled pleasure he takes in giving us the kingdom. "Fear not, little flock, for it is your Father's *pleasure* to give you the kingdom."[8]

God is a happy God who does not act beyond His own perfect desires. He is good and He does good.[9] If He loves you, it is not because He had to be convinced to do so. He is not in heaven

---

8. John Piper, *The Pleasures of God: Meditations on God's Delight in Being God* (Multnomah Books, 2000), 305.
9. Psalm 119:68.

fighting feelings of disdain for you. He sent His Son to lay down His life for you because He wanted to. God is not like us in that He can be bribed or convinced or coerced to do something He doesn't want to do. His ways are pure and holy and just and good. When He saved you, it was because He delighted to save you. You do not have to now *convince* Him to keep loving you. He has already loved you with the kind of love that He has for His own Son.[10] And His love endures forever.[11] If you are in Christ, you do not have to fear God's thoughts about you.

> To be known by God is to be loved by Him.

I gave a list of verses from Psalms that speak to God's pleasure in His people. I could give another list of verses also from Psalms that speaks to God's displeasure in sinners, in His actual hatred toward evildoers. Scripture does not mince words about how God feels about sin. But the difference between the evildoers He hates and the righteous He loves is the very core of this entire book. The difference comes in being known by God.

In the book of Nahum, the prophet declares that "the LORD is good, a stronghold in the day of trouble; he knows those who take refuge in him" (Nah. 1:7). What separates those who find refuge in the Lord from those who incur judgment from Him is being *known* by him. As we've discussed throughout this book, to be known by God is to be loved by Him. And love isn't hard for Him. We tend to believe that because we still struggle with sin, therefore God must still struggle to love us. We fear He must have to work so very hard to love someone who is so very unlovable. But this isn't the picture we get from Scripture. He's better at love

10. John 15:9.
11. Psalm 136.

than we can ever hope to be, for He Himself is the source of it.[12] He can correct our sin while still delighting to call us His own.

GOD'S THOUGHTS GIVE OUR LIVES MEANING

I love that David uses Psalm 139:17–18 as an exclamatory pause. After extolling God's knowledge, presence, and care, it's as though David needed to interject his amazement before moving on. God's thoughts are so other and so numerous as to be beyond human comprehension. It is good to dwell on Him this way. Psalm 92:5 mirrors the exclamation of verse 17: "How great are your works, O LORD! Your thoughts are very deep!" We're meant to consider the vastness of God's mind and, like the psalmists, rejoice in it. His depth of knowledge sits in stark contrast to our own limited version, which the Lord knows is "but a breath" (Ps. 94:11).

This section of Psalm 139 should shape our thoughts of God as well as how we live our lives before Him. We should pause and wonder at His greatness like David. We should take time to let that spiritual sonder settle over us anew as we remember how glorious He is. We should go to sleep and wake up knowing He faithfully kept us all night long because He loves us. We should also let His wise, innumerable thoughts take precedence over man's thoughts—including our own.

Paul tells us that "the wisdom of this world is folly with God" (1 Cor. 3:19). The best offerings of this world in art and business and science and literature and music pale in comparison with God's wisdom and creativity. A legacy that presses that tombstone dash with meaning will be one that serves His kingdom purposes, not our own. Nor that of other people. In our efforts to make our lives matter, we must do so with an eye on eternity.

12. 1 John 4:16.

Man's opinions are fickle and stained by sin. Our opinions are fickle and stained by sin. God's thoughts, however, are pure. His opinion is most important, and His purposes will stand forever.

Consider God's vast knowledge and wonder at His greatness as David did. And then rejoice because He thinks of you with love and care just as He has with every saint throughout all of history. It's not hard for Him! Just as no one who belongs to Him will be lost, He won't let our lives float away on the wind without meaning.[13] If He has set His faithful love on you, your life will always matter to Him. And that's enough for any tombstone.

It is human nature to seek notoriety or uniqueness. We don't want to be reduced to forgotten dashes in lonely cemeteries. But the cure for this fear isn't to build lives that scream our uniqueness and individualism on this earth. In the end, we'll still face death and be forgotten by others. Man's thoughts are limited and his affections fickle. But God's aren't. The longing to be unique and remembered is, at its core, a desire to be known and loved by someone who won't forget us. "We need to know that someone sees us as so special and so precious that their minds are dominated with us."[14] This is why God's thoughts of us matter the most. It's why God's mindfulness of us in Psalm 8 outweighs anything we could build for ourselves or our own names in this life.

Being image bearers means our lives must be connected to God for us to really find purpose and meaning. Tim Keller writes, "'To be in the image' means that human beings were not created to stand alone. We must get our significance and security from something of ultimate value outside us. To be created in God's image means we must live for the true God or we will have to

---

13. John 10:28.
14. Dr. Timothy Keller, "The Search for Identity" on Psalm 8, of the series "Modern Problems, Ancient Solutions" preached at Redeemer Presbyterian Church on October 10, 1993.

make something else God and orbit our lives around that."[15] It is *God* who gives us meaning and purpose, and until we grasp that, we'll look for ways to make our mark that will only be fleeting and futile. When we are certain of the Lord's affection for us, however, we can worry less about being remembered in this life and instead build our lives around what will last forever. We will be remembered by God because even when we die, we will be with Him forever.

We can live small lives of ordinary faithfulness, fighting sin and loving God, because He knows our names and will never forget us.

In light of this, we can delay gratification in this life and focus on what will last forever—what lasts far beyond those tombstone dashes. Randy Alcorn writes,

> When we realize the pleasures that await us in God's presence, we can forgo lesser pleasures now. When we realize the possessions that await us in Heaven, we will gladly give away possessions on Earth to store up treasures in Heaven. When we realize the power offered to us as rulers in God's Kingdom, a power we could not handle now but will handle with humility and benevolence then, we can forgo the pursuit of power here.[16]

We do not have to work so hard to make a mark on this earth in order to be known and remembered. We can live small lives of ordinary faithfulness, fighting sin and loving God, because He knows our names and will never forget us. We can live for our

---

15. Timothy Keller, *Rediscovering Jonah: The Secret of God's Mercy* (Penguin Books, 2020), 49.

16. Randy Alcorn, *Heaven* (Tyndale House Publishers, 2004), 471.

eternal city whose builder and architect is God, knowing that He will never forget or forsake us for He is not ashamed to know us.[17]

My chiropractor-grandfather and my grandmother spent their retirement years serving with the Tennessee Baptists disaster relief team. Whenever a hurricane or earthquake struck, my grandparents traveled to serve food all day for many weeks at a time. My grandmother who documented World War II lived to be ninety-six and spent decades of her life discipling young women to follow Jesus. My mom and dad housed single moms in their home when they could have been empty-nesters, and they continue to serve the Lord in their church and community. My brother and sister seek to glorify God in their work as good employees who steward their gifts faithfully. Being known and loved by God shapes our innate desires to matter into desires that matter for *eternity*.

The notoriety or uniqueness doesn't matter so much in light of that tombstone dash. The faithfulness does.

KNOWN AND REMEMBERED

What are God's thoughts of you? They are thoughts of love and faithfulness and mercy. They are shaping and molding and growing. God has good thoughts of you. Go ahead and try to count them. When you fall asleep, know that He is faithfully awake, keeping watch over your soul. When you wake up, He is there. You're still with Him, and He still loves you. He'll always love you. He'll always remember you, for how could He forget the ones whom He has saved and redeemed? He could no more forget you than a mother forgets her nursing child. He could no more forget you than He could forget the scars in His hands.[18]

The dashes on our future tombstones can't capture all of

17. Hebrews 11:16.
18. Isaiah 49:15–16.

God's thoughts of us. The sins you have fought in your life don't define His thoughts of you. Neither do the good things you have worked to achieve in this life—not ultimately. Here's what matters about your life in the end: You were dead in your sins but He made you alive. He loved you while you were still a sinner. His thoughts of you are bright with the radiance of His Son, whose righteousness covers you like a warm blanket. You'll be known and forever loved because He died for you.

That says more about who you are than any tombstone ever could.

○   ○   ○

for further thought:

1. What do you learn about God's character from Psalm 139:17–18?

2. In what ways have you tried to leave a legacy that will last beyond your earthly life? Is it inherently wrong to want to be remembered? Why or why not?

3. How can you delay gratification in this life and live for what will matter for eternity? Give some examples related to work, creativity, and/or relationships.

4. Paul tells us in 2 Corinthians 5:16–21 that we have been made new creatures in Christ and that we are "the righteousness of God." How should that inform your belief about God's thoughts toward you?

5. Read Hebrews 11:13–16. What is our calling as faithful citizens of heaven?

PSALM
139:19–22

Oh that you would slay the wicked, O God!
O men of blood, depart from me!
They speak against you with malicious intent;
your enemies take your name in vain.
Do I not hate those who hate you, O LORD?
And do I not loathe those who rise up against
you?
I hate them with complete hatred;
I count them my enemies.

Search me, O God, and know my heart!
Try me and know my thoughts!
And see if there be any grievous way in me,
and lead me in the way everlasting!

7

Known When the World Is Against You

Should I Hate God's Enemies?

My husband and I celebrated our twentieth wedding anniversary in Maine where we had honeymooned two decades prior. We spent one warm day wandering around downtown Portland, and as the day wore on, we had trouble finding a place to eat lunch. It was summertime, and Portland was packed with tourists; all the restaurants had long lines and wait times.

Growing hungrier and warmer by the moment, we walked several blocks looking for a place with air conditioning and an open table. We came upon a restaurant with a curious name and a lovely outdoor seating area. As we stepped into the restaurant, it took a few minutes for our eyes to adjust to the dark interior. The room was large with dark corner booths and a scrubby looking bar. Everything was painted black and looked a bit worn down, giving the place a seedy feeling. The restaurant was completely empty at 12:30 on a Thursday afternoon during peak tourist season.

Before we could turn around and head back outside into the sunshine, the restaurant host materialized from a dark hallway and greeted us. He wore a Hawaiian shirt that seemed wildly out of place with his surroundings. "Two?" he asked while grabbing a couple of menus. My husband hesitated and glanced at me. Feeling my blood sugar plummeting, I nodded. I just needed to eat. The host steered us deeper into the dark, empty restaurant. He guided us to a large dark staircase and began walking up the steps. Reluctantly, we followed. Midway up the staircase, my husband turned around to face me with a troubled look on his face. "Where is he taking us?" he mouthed, eyes wide. I did not understand why the host had passed dozens of empty tables on the ground floor. Why was he taking us upstairs? *What* was upstairs? (Was this a trap?)

When we reached the top of the stairs, we stepped into a room bathed in light. Floor-to-ceiling windows opened the room to a view of the Portland harbor. The room was as stunning as the view. Coastal hued shiplap, white tablecloths, a profusion of flowers, and flickering candles on every table. This seemed like a totally different restaurant. The host seated us at a small table next to the windows where we ate the best food of our trip and watched boats drift in and out of the harbor. Seagulls swooped by, fishermen loaded up their skiffs, and harbor tour ships loaded and unloaded passengers. We watched it all from our beautiful table in that beautiful room on the top floor of the most confusing restaurant I've ever visited.

When we finished our meal and descended that dark staircase to the ground floor, the difference between the two rooms was jarring. I later looked up the restaurant on travel websites and found five-star reviews from confused diners. *Great food. That upstairs, though! What is going on with this restaurant?* This place had an identity crisis. But somehow, that strange, dark, dank downstairs made the upper level more beautiful for the confusing path it took to get there. Somehow, it made sense.

A PSALM WITH AN IDENTITY CRISIS?

Thus far, Psalm 139 has painted a beautiful portrait of a God who knows everything and loves deeply. He is profoundly *other* and deeply personal. Reflecting on His personal care, we regard this psalm as comfort for the insecure and the uncertain. And, stylistically, it's beautiful. You can feel your view of God expanding as you meditate on the words.

But then you get to verse 19. The change in tone, content, and style is so jarring that you're not even sure you're in the same psalm you've been reading for eighteen verses. The tone shifts from exaltation and adoration to hatred and contempt. Verses 19–22 fall into the genre of *imprecatory poetry*, and they seem wildly out of place.

Like the restaurant in Maine that didn't seem to know what it was, Psalm 139 appears to shift from a poetic masterpiece about God's omniscience and love to a vengeful proclamation that calls for the death of His enemies. Does this psalm have an identity crisis? Why did David steer us in this direction? How do we get back to the verses full of light and harbor views?

THE CURSING PSALMS

Imprecatory prayers pepper the Bible's large book of poetry. You can find them in Psalms 5, 10, 17, 35, 58, 59, 69, 70, 79, 83, 109, 129, 137, 140, and yes—even Psalm 139. Often called "the hate psalms" or "the cursing psalms," these prayers unsettle us when we read them through our modern eyes. Writer Greg Morse defines imprecatory psalms this way: "The imprecatory psalms, then, are not direct curses upon the wicked apart from the Almighty. They are *prayers* offered and entrusted to the wisdom and enforcement of the psalmist's covenant God."[1] Imprecatory psalms ask the Lord to enact judgment that is perfectly just.

In other words, imprecatory psalms are prayers that God would bring about the things that are already promised to happen to those who continually reject Him as Lord. They are prayed in tandem with God's will and His Word. Morse gives a helpful example to explain: "The statement of fact given in Psalm 1, 'The wicked . . . are like chaff that the wind drives away' (Psalm 1:4) becomes for David, '*Let them be* like chaff before the wind' (Psalm 35:5)."[2]

We see something similar in Psalm 139:19. David prays, "Oh that you would slay the wicked, O God!" It sounds vindictive, doesn't it? But he is simply praying for God to bring about what is already promised about those who perpetuate wickedness and reject God. Psalm 9:17 (among other places in Scripture) dictates the dire future of those who refuse to worship God, saying that "the wicked will return to Sheol, all the nations that forget God." Sheol, as we've discussed, is a reference to the grave. Death. *The end.* David prays in Psalm 139:19 that God would bring about the decisive end that awaits those who reject God.

But why would David do this? Why now in this jarring section of verses near the end of what has been a beautifully constructed psalm of adoration? Did he ruin it? These verses are difficult to reconcile with the rest of the psalm:

Oh that you would slay the wicked, O God! O men of blood, depart from me! They speak against you with a malicious intent; your enemies take your name in vain. Do I

---

1. Greg Morse, "'Oh Slay the Wicked': How Christians Sing Curses," *Desiring God*, September 6, 2023, https://www.desiringgod.org/articles/oh-slay-the-wicked.
2. Morse, "Oh Slay the Wicked."

not hate those who hate you, O LORD? And do I not loathe those who rise up against you? I hate them with complete hatred; I count them my enemies.

Complete hatred? It's tempting to assume that this portion of Psalm 139 is not for us. We could easily be convinced to skip it and move on to the next and more positive section. We're new covenant believers in Jesus, after all. We're supposed to love our enemies, not hate them with complete hatred! Imprecatory psalms were for the Old Testament saints. We can just skip to the good part, right?

There are many scholars whom I deeply respect who would agree with the above statements. They believe we can learn from the imprecatory psalms, but we shouldn't pray them. But did you know that every time you pray, "Come, Lord Jesus, come!" you're praying in an imprecatory manner?[3]

When you pray for Christ to return, you're asking Him to return and vanquish all His foes, sending all of those who have rejected Him straight to the fires of hell. That's what we learn will happen throughout the book of Revelation, after all. When Jesus returns to resurrect those who have died in faith and take them home along with the living Christians, He will also exact judgment on the wicked.

> *The picture we get of the end of the wicked is difficult to swallow. Yet we long for Jesus to return and pray for His coming to be near, don't we? We long to see Him return and set things right.*

---

3. Trevin Wax, "What C. S. Lewis Got Wrong About the Cursing Psalms," *The Gospel Coalition*, March 21, 2023, https://www.thegospelcoalition.org/blogs/trevin-wax/cs-lewis-cursing-psalms/.

The wrath of God against those who've rejected Jesus as King will be absolute, and it will be final. It will also be gruesome in its reach. John writes that the blood that flows from the winepress of God's wrath will flow roughly 184 miles long and nearly as deep as a horse is tall.[4]

That changes things a little, doesn't it? The picture we get of the end of the wicked is difficult to swallow. Yet we *long* for Jesus to return and pray for His coming to be near, don't we? I know I do. I long to see Him return and set things right. I long for Him to put an end to sin, to decisively shut down Satan's deception, to stop the influence of those who revile His name. In my heart, I long to see the King of kings reign forever in the new creation. But I can't pray for His return without praying for the end of the wicked. The one will lead to the other.

And yet, I think of unsaved friends, family members, and neighbors who have thus far rejected Christ. I do not want them to be included in those who incur God's righteous judgment for sin. I want them to run to the cross, to plead the name of Jesus for salvation. And I want them to do it soon. Long before Jesus returns and it's too late.

This is the delicate line we walk as believers in Jesus. We pray for God's justice, but we also pray for His salvation. We pray for the lost to come to faith, but we pray for God to right the grievous wrongs that humans have inflicted upon one another by bringing it to an end. We pray for mercy *and* we pray for justice. This is what it means to be known and loved by God. It means identifying with God and aligning ourselves with His will and His word. It means loving what He loves and hating what He hates. Sometimes, it means praying with an imprecatory bent. After all, Jesus did.

4. Revelation 14:20.

IMPRECATORY KINDNESS

In the gospel of John, Jesus quotes twice from an imprecatory psalm. In John 2:14–17, Jesus cleansed the temple with a whip and a determination to drive out the moneychangers who were both profiting off the backs of worshipers and keeping non-Jewish worshipers out of the temple. Jesus took strong action against them, fulfilling the words of Psalm 69: "Zeal for your house has consumed me." Later, in His instructions to the disciples to abide in Him and keep His commandments, Jesus warns them about coming persecution. Again, pulling from Psalm 69, Jesus identified as the one who was persecuted "without cause," preparing His friends for the hatred of the world (John 15:25). If the world hated Jesus, it would surely hate His followers.

And herein lies our connection to the imprecatory psalms as friends and disciples of Jesus. Through faith in His sacrifice at the cross, through His propitiation for our sin, through the miraculous exchange of our sin for His righteousness, we are now included in the people of God. We no longer identify with the wicked who have rejected Him, though that is who we used to be. But now we have been made righteous—indeed we *are* the righteousness of God through Christ![5] That means that we identify with Him in both suffering and our perception of the world. We love what He loves. We hate what He hates. We want to see people from all nations turn to Him in faith, and we trust that God will exact judgment on those who don't. Don't miss the way that last sentence was worded, though. *God* will exact judgment. Not us. We are not the ones seeking vengeance. Rather, we trust the *Lord* to make things right when the time is right. He alone will do it with equity and righteousness, His actions unstained by sin.

---

5. 2 Corinthians 5:21.

The apostle Paul tells us to bless those who persecute us and act kindly toward them.[6] In the very same paragraph, he tells us why we can do this: "Never avenge yourselves, but leave it to the wrath of God, for it is written, 'Vengeance is mine, I will repay, says the Lord'" (Rom. 12:19, quoting Deut. 32:35). Read those words again and closely. This is both kindness and imprecation. This is how Christians are to think toward those who persecute them, who hate God and those who associate with His name. Don't avenge yourself. Trust God to take care of it with His wrath. In the meantime, be kind to those who come against you. Paul braids the imprecatory prayer for God to avenge the wicked in His righteous wrath with the command to love and bless those who are mistreating us for our faith in Jesus.

It's so upside-down. Love and mercy meet truth and justice. This is the Christian way.

DAVID WASN'T WRONG

Let's go back to Psalm 139:19–22. David desires for God to slay (kill!) the wicked, the ones who speak against God with malicious intent. He hates them—for they hate God. He loathes them for setting themselves up against this God who has set His love and affection on David. He counts as his enemies those who hate the God he loves. It sounds harsh, but after looking at the first eighteen verses outlining God's tender care for David, there is something right about his desire for the demise of those who have the gall to pit themselves against such a wonderous, kind, intensely loving God.

You're not so far from imprecatory prayers yourself. Think about it. How do you feel when you see injustice in this world?

6. Romans 12:14, 20.

When you read the news and see reports of ethnic-based eugenics in China or when extremists burn down churches in Nigeria, your heart swells with righteous anger. You *know* this is an affront to God who has created all people in His image, and you pray for the Lord to bring the wicked to a swift end. This is imprecatory. You also pray for missionaries to take the gospel to the lost and for persecuted saints to speak the words of Christ to any who will hear. This is kindness. And this is how we who sit on this side of the redemptive story of Scripture should understand David's jarring prayer in Psalm 139. Justice *and* mercy.

We pray for Him to return and end injustice for the sake of His name, but we also pray that these same souls will bend their knees and cry out to Him for forgiveness and redemption.

We know that people who spit on the name of Christ and revel in their sin have pridefully pitted themselves against the Creator who crafted them with care in their mother's womb. We feel the roiling anger of injustice as they smear His name and bow down to the altar of sin and self. We pray for Him to return and end this for the sake of His name, but we also pray that these same souls will bend their knees and cry out to Him for forgiveness and redemption. We pray this because, as Paul reminds us, "And such were some of you." So was I. And you. "But you were washed, you were sanctified, you were justified in the name of the Lord Jesus Christ and by the Spirit of our God" (1 Cor. 6:11).

Who you are now is not who you used to be before Jesus made you new. But now you *are* new, so you must think like one who is new, one who has been washed and justified and sanctified. Your attitude toward injustice and wickedness and idolatry cannot be indifference. We're known and loved. We identify with God. His enemies are our enemies. His purposes are our purposes. His loves are our loves. We live to glorify the name of the Lord, so we must respond to evil rightly. We respond as Jesus did by loving our enemies and praying for them.[7] And we respond like Jesus by longing for the Father to be glorified in all the earth.[8] He is not glorified by sinful, wicked injustice.

MY IMPRECATORY PRAYER

My church has an interesting story. Formerly a predominantly White Baptist church and a predominantly Black Methodist church, our body of believers merged in 2019 to form one ethnically diverse, gospel-centered church in a poor, underserved area of our quite segregated city. Jim Crow laws might have dissolved with the Civil Rights Movement, but our town still struggles with race relations and integration—especially in worship. Our church, led by the wisdom and love of two faithful pastors, is seeking to bridge the racial divide with the unifying gospel of Jesus. We purchased land in the neighborhood where we meet for worship with the intent to build a community center that will eventually house our church and provide after-school programs, job training, a laundromat, and affordable daycare to the neighborhood.

Because our story is unique, the local news station and newspapers advertised our groundbreaking ceremony and showed up with a decent crowd. We were excited that day! We were watching the Lord answer years of prayers in how to get the gospel to our neighborhood while meeting practical needs. It was to be a momentous day in our church's history. So you can imagine

7. Matthew 5:43–45.
8. Matthew 6:9–10.

my shock when I noticed a middle-aged couple with clipboards milling among the crowd seeking signatures to overturn good, strict abortion laws in our state.[9] Not only were they hijacking our celebratory event to garner support for their agenda, they were not even from our city. They had targeted a poor, diverse neighborhood to push an abominable practice that is completely out of step with our ministry. I was furious.

Ordinarily leery of conflict, I marched up to the couple and asked them to leave. They insisted they had every right to be there in a public space. "But," I pushed back, "this is not *your* event. This isn't right what you're doing." They ignored me and started working the crowd. I stayed close, not letting anyone get near them without my presence. I overheard a group of women from the neighborhood discussing it. "Isn't this the church's event? I guess they invited those people."

My pastor-husband kindly (and with less frustration than me) asked the couple to stop canvassing. When they argued, he said they were welcome to stay but to please stop asking for signatures. I watched them closely and, eventually, they left.

The event was spoiled for me, though. I wrestled with the motives of that couple all night long. My emotions thinned, stretching out in two very different directions. Part of me wanted swift justice to end their efforts. "Lord, cut off the arm of the wicked!" I prayed while I tossed and turned in bed. But the other part of me knew that without Christ I might be following a similar path. The only thing that separates me from those who love what God hates is the transforming power of the gospel. So my prayer shifted: "Lord,

9. Abortion denigrates God's design and value of human life. As we discussed in chapter 5, every human is created in the image of God and therefore holds inherent value. To fight for the right to end the life of an image bearer is to disbelieve the Bible's affirmation of the inherent dignity and value of human life.

please save them and open their eyes to the truth of Christ!"

I wanted their actions to cease. I wanted them to be reconciled to God. I wanted God to do whatever it took to bring both prayers to reality. This was my imprecatory prayer.

As I prayed for God to keep my heart soft toward those who hate what He loves and love what He hates, I suddenly understood the need for imprecatory prayers *and* prayers for the lost to be saved. For the Christian it's not either/or. It's both/and. It's justice and love. It's God's vengeance and God's mercy. It's praying for the wicked to repent and for God to end their rebellion. It's a desire for the name of the Knower and Lover to be revered over all the earth, in our entire city, throughout our church's neighborhood, in the heart of every image bearer.

KNOWN AND INCLUDED

David's prayer is jarring when we first read it. But it's not out of place. It's not a dark, dank dive bar beneath a beautiful fine dining restaurant with harbor views. His psalm doesn't have an identity crisis. David wasn't confused. The first eighteen verses give us the scaffolding we need in order to look up and rightly see the imprecatory prayer. We've looked at God's character, at His gracious, personal care for us. We've exalted Him for being so kind, for never abandoning us or treating us as our sins deserve. We've praised Him for looking at us and seeing Jesus. We rejoice because we who were far off have been brought near and included in His family.

If God has known and loved us so deeply and intimately, then His knowledge and care have bearing on our lives. We are His. Belonging to Him means identifying with Him. We identify with Christ in His suffering, and we identify with God as the One who rules the universe and rightly deserves the worship of every bowed knee and every confessing tongue. So when we don't see it come to pass, we should yearn for His kingdom to come on earth as it has in heaven. We should recoil with righteous anger when human life is treated without dignity. We should grieve when we see the name of the Lord defamed and reviled.

We have climbed up and seen the harbor views of God's wondrous character and His steadfast care for our souls. So we must long for all the world to see Him as He truly is. We must yearn for all people to repent rather than to revile. We should hunger for the day when King Jesus the Righteous comes to set things right for good. So we pray. We pray for Him to come, and we pray for people to repent. And we speak the name of the great Knower and Lover to all who will listen so that they too will be swept up in the never-ending love of God.

○ ○ ○

for further thought:

1. How have you thought about the imprecatory psalms in the past? Have you ever felt the need or desire to pray them?

2. Read Psalm 3:7. What does David say that God does for his enemies? Now read Psalm 58:6. How does this imprecatory prayer follow the path of praying according to God's will?

3. What do you learn about God from Psalm 139:19–22?

4. How does praying imprecatory prayers with a gospel lens protect us from sinful hatred of our enemies?

5. How can you pray for those who have hurt you or who have reviled your faith in Jesus?

Oh that you would slay the wicked, O God!
    O men of blood, depart from me!
They speak against you with malicious intent;
    your enemies take your name in vain.
Do I not hate those who hate you, O LORD?
    And do I not loathe those who rise up against
        you?
I hate them with complete hatred;
    I count them my enemies.

**PSALM
139:23–24**

Search me, O God, and know my heart!
    Try me and know my thoughts!
And see if there be any grievous way in me,
    and lead me in the way everlasting!

8

Known and Kept

What if I Fear Falling Away?

The car rental company gave us a minivan. My husband and I had just landed in Oakland, California, with my sister and brother-in-law for five days of exploring the California coastline. A group of forty-somethings, we were the epitome of *cool* as we piled our luggage into the black Honda Odyssey and headed for the airport exit.

A kind gate attendant gave us directions from her enclosed booth, but her words didn't quite match her smile: "Turn left and then right before heading toward San Francisco. But *whatever* you do, do not stop on Hegenberger Road. Do not stop for gas, do not get out of your vehicle, do not roll down your windows. I'm telling you, whatever you do, *do not stop on that road.* Okay! Have a great trip—and welcome to California!" She waved and smiled at the four of us in the minivan. Mouths agape, we watched her close her booth window and raise the bar for our exit.

We did have to drive down Hegenberger Road to leave the city and get to the smaller, safer town where we were staying, but you can be sure we did not stop. The gate attendant's words echoed all week on our trip. We didn't know what lay behind her warnings, but we nervously laughed about her words all week long. "You probably shouldn't be here—but welcome and good luck!"

"WELCOME. I AM WITH YOU"

Psalm 139 closes with David's plea for God to keep on knowing him. "Search me, O God, and know my heart! Try me and know my thoughts!" Notice the shift in tense. In verse 1, David praises God because He has *already* searched and known him—past tense. Here, David asks (or demands) that He *continue* to do so—now and in the future. The imperative structure of the sentences further drives home David's intent. He wants God to keep His commitment to care for him and guide him in the way he should go. He begs the Lord to keep him on the right path forever.

What we learn from David's prayer is that God is not like a well-intentioned gate attendant who welcomes you and wishes you good luck without elaborating about what lies ahead. He doesn't welcome us into His family and then leave us to figure out the Christian life on our own. He continually knows our hearts, reveals our sin, guides us in the way we should go, and makes us more like Jesus.

This process is what Christians call *sanctification*. It's the window of time in your life between your salvation (when you came to faith in Jesus) and your glorification (when you see Him face to face and are unable to sin). In that window of time, God molds you more and more into the image of His Son because He didn't just commit to save you but also to grow and shape you. He uses His Word, His church, His Spirit, and all kinds of trials and circumstances in life to keep us near His side.[1] He "works all things

---

1. For a fuller treatment of sanctification, check out my book *Everyday Faithfulness: The Beauty of Ordinary Perseverance in a Demanding World* (Crossway, 2020).

according to the counsel of his will," which means He will do in our lives what is for our good and for His glory (Eph. 1:11). He is committed to you, your growth, and His glory in your life. God's involvement in your life didn't end with your salvation. His love for you didn't end at the cross. It goes on and on and on. With God, it isn't "Welcome and good luck!" It's "Welcome. I am with you." Even, Jesus told us, "to the end of the age" (Matt. 28:20).

THOUGHTS, CARES, AND SINS

"Try me and know my thoughts!" David writes in verse 23. You could translate "thoughts" as "cares." Whatever it is you're thinking or concerned about, you can, like David, ask the Lord to sift it. You can ask Him to reveal anything that doesn't need to be there and to carry anything that's too heavy for you to bear. Peter gives us similar instructions: "Humble yourselves, therefore, under the mighty hand of God so that at the proper time he may exalt you, casting all your anxieties on him, because he cares for you" (1 Peter 5:6–7).

Peter connects the freeing release of our anxieties with God's personal care for us. You can throw your fears and concerns onto His shoulders *because* He loves you. The ability to "cast" your anxieties on the Lord, however, requires that you flee from sin and resist the enemy's temptations.[2] As we've discussed, God's love for us doesn't make room for ongoing sin in our lives. Peter exhorts us to be humble before the Lord. David asks God to reveal his sin (Ps. 139:24). Both desire the Lord to sift their thoughts and carry their concerns.

To walk securely in God's love, you must reckon with the sin in your heart. Sin is deceiving and will tell you all sorts of lies

2. 1 Peter 5:8.

about God and yourself. But be sure of this: God loves you too much to let you wander away from Him. He carries your burdens, but He also corrects your sin. As often as we pray for Him to take the anxious thoughts we carry, we should also pray for Him to reveal the areas of sin we've missed.

Show Me My Sin

David prays, "And see if there be any grievous way in me," petitioning God to reveal any sin lurking in his heart that would affect his relationship with the Lord. He appeals to God's omniscience, depending on Him to see what David can't, to know what David has missed, to expose what David had hidden—either intentionally or not.

Asking God to reveal our sin is a right prayer and one we ought to pray regularly. We are not all-knowing the way God is, and we are not always the best judges of ourselves. The author of Hebrews tells us that the deceitful nature of sin can harden our hearts, blinding us to our true condition.[3] When our hearts are hardened by sin, we wander from the faith with little idea or care of the danger beyond the path of righteousness.

My husband and I took our kids on a hike not too long ago, and before we hit the trail, we warned both of our sons to stay on the path at all times. The woods were filled with poison ivy, and one of my sons is quite the explorer. (Actually, he's a "runner"— you know, the kid who sprints across a parking lot without ever checking for cars.) About an hour into our hike and an hour away from the trailhead, my young runner strayed from the path to grab a large stick from what appeared to be a small ditch. As he reached for the stick, in went his foot, and he sank up to his

---

3. Hebrews 3:13.

knee in stiff, wet Missouri clay. My husband and I joined forces to pull him out, but his foot came up out of the mud without the shoe. We pulled the shoe out with the stick (the one that was so alluring in the first place), and my son had to bear the natural consequences of walking with a clay-encrusted leg all the way back to the trailhead.

Sin is deceitful like that. While most of us are aware of the obvious danger to our souls from things like pornography or theft, we're not always as conscientious or vigilant about the harm caused by envy and pride or anger and resentment. And even with the more obvious or blatant areas of sin, we're not always inclined to say "no." We're not impervious to sin's deceit, and even the smallest steps away from the path of righteousness can bring about a lot of heartache and painful consequences.

In our lack of omniscience, it is for our spiritual safety and personal holiness that we ask God to show us our sins, to "see if there be any grievous way" in us. We need to keep a right view of who God is—holy and glorious and mighty and kind—but our sin can block the light of His glory from our eyes. And sometimes we don't even know it. So, we pray like David. We ask God to reveal our sin and help us to burn it to the ground. We plead for His help and we accept His means of correction.

God isn't wishing us luck on this sanctification journey. He is with us every step of the way. He has provided what we need to stay on His path of righteousness.[4] He has given us His Word to guide us, His church to protect, correct, and comfort us, and His Spirit to help us understand Scripture and obey it. When you pray for God to help you see and fight your sin, you must use the weapons He has provided.

---

4. 2 Peter 1:3–11.

We must see God's love as corrective, not permissive. We must also see His correction as love, not as punishment.

Discipline and Delight

I used to think that God was mad at me when I sinned and happy with me when I didn't. I gauged His affections by my actions, attributing to Him the up-and-down roller coaster of emotions like any wishy-washy human who is easily peeved and put out. But God is not like us. And He is not manipulated by my good or bad actions.

God is constant in His love and faithful in His deeds. He is ever steady. If He disciplines us to eradicate sin in our lives, it isn't because He's mad at us. On the contrary, it's because He loves us. Discipline isn't punitive if you have been saved through faith in Jesus. Paul says in Romans 8 that there is "no condemnation for those who are in Christ Jesus" (Rom. 8:1). This is a critical point of our theology of salvation. If Jesus swallowed all of God's wrath at the cross, then there is no more punishment for you to bear in addition to that. No penance. No making it up to God. No serving out of debt, for your record of debt has been nailed to the cross and canceled.[5]

Discipline, on the other hand, is something God does to help us live far from sin. Keeping our lives unstained by the world leads to greater joy and perseverance in Christ. God knows what we need. He knows what tempts us. He knows all the little and big areas in our lives that squelch and smother our obedience to Him. So He disciplines us to bring us closer. He uses the sorrows and trials of this life to purify our faith into something strong and true.

5. Colossians 2:14.

If He hated you, He would not bother refining your faith.

The author of Hebrews talks about the Lord's discipline as part of our sanctification process. But it's done from the point of view of God as our Father. "He disciplines us for our good, that we may share his holiness," the author says (Heb. 12:10). "God is treating you as sons" (Heb. 12:7). But it isn't that picture of an angry, grumpy father we talked about earlier in this book. No, this is a good Father we're talking about. This is a compassionate Father. This is a Father who runs to greet the prodigal son and clothes his filth with a clean robe of righteousness.

God is the perfect Father who disciplines from perfect love.

Quoting Proverbs 3, the author of Hebrews urges us not to be weary or discouraged when the Lord disciplines us. Rather—view it as love. Proverbs 3 says that "the LORD reproves him whom he *loves*, as a father the son in whom he *delights*" (Prov. 3:12).[6] God delights in His children, so He disciplines them to protect them from further sin and to help them grow in holiness. Unlike our imperfect parenting where we snip and berate our kids for muddy shoes and deliberate disobedience, God corrects from a place of perfect love. Without snippiness or mean-spiritedness or selfishness. Regardless of how golden or bleak our experience with earthly parents, we must avoid embedding human flaws into God's parenting of our souls. He is the perfect Father who disciplines from perfect love.

If God is revealing areas of sin in your life as you have prayed for Him to do—and if you feel crushed by the weight of it—do not run from God. Do not accuse Him of not loving you for

---

6. I must credit my husband, William, for connecting this idea of delight and discipline in his sermon on Proverbs 3:1–12, titled "Wisdom Is Obedience," preached at Grace Bible Fellowship on August 11, 2024.

the misery you feel under the spotlight of correction. Do not attribute to Him what you yourself tend to do in anger. Rather, accept His discipline. Receive the rebukes of Scripture and cherish the correction of faithful church members and pastors. View discipline as God loving you enough to pluck you from the Missouri mud pit and setting you on the path again by His side. He is keeping you.

Don't resist His discipline. But don't feel condemned by it either.

WHAT ABOUT THE WARNING PASSAGES?

Maybe you don't resist God's discipline. Maybe you are constantly aware of it, welcoming it because the only way you can categorize your relationship with the Lord is "guilt-ridden." While we've already discussed the struggle with shame and guilt for past and present sins in chapter 3, there are undoubtedly readers who live with fear of falling away. They struggle to believe in God's faithful love and affection because they live in constant fear of Scripture's sobering warning passages.

If that's you, I want you to know that ultimately, you are the reason I wrote this book.

You're the one who lives with your sin ever before you (Ps. 51:3) but doesn't believe God willingly upholds you (Ps. 51:12). You don't doubt God's general love, but you are so certain you qualify as a potential apostate that you live your whole Christian life with regular, crushing condemnation. You're sure that if you let in even a glimmer of God's approval, you'll probably give yourself license to sin and eventually fall away. To anyone who pushes back against your bleak view of God's love, you are armed with a stack of warnings against apostasy. Fear is your shield, and doubt is your sword. But they'll crumble if you realize you're giving yourself too much credit for your faithfulness to Jesus. You're not solely responsible for keeping on the path of righteousness. The Lord is the One who keeps you on the way everlasting.

"But! But the warning passages!" you argue. Well, let's talk about that. The warning passages are indeed sobering. Consider these (if you haven't already learned them by heart):

> "Nevertheless, with most of them God was not pleased, for they were overthrown in the wilderness. Now these things took place as examples for us, that we might not desire evil as they did. . . . Therefore let anyone who thinks that he stands take heed lest he fall." (1 Cor. 10:5–6, 12)

> "Therefore we must pay much closer attention to what we have heard, lest we drift away from it. . . . How shall we escape if we neglect such a great salvation?" (Heb. 2:1, 3)

> "Take care, brothers, lest there be in any of you an evil, unbelieving heart, leading you to fall away from the living God." (Heb. 3:12)

> "Therefore, while the promise of entering his rest still stands, let us fear lest any of you should seem to have failed to reach it." (Heb. 4:1)

> "For it is impossible, in the case of those who have once been enlightened . . . and then have fallen away, to restore them again to repentance, since they are crucifying once again the Son of God to their own harm and holding him up to contempt." (Heb. 6:4, 6)

> "For if we go on sinning deliberately after receiving the knowledge of the truth, there no longer remains a sacrifice

for sins. . . . How much worse punishment, do you think, will be deserved by the one who has trampled underfoot the Son of God, and has profaned the blood of the covenant by which he was sanctified, and has outraged the Spirit of grace?" (Heb. 10:26, 29)

Perhaps just seeing those verses ignites fear in your heart. It's good for us to read with reverence for God. Walking away from faith in Christ and from the truth of Scripture is a dangerous, dangerous thing. But if you live in constant fear that you'll fall away, you might be misreading those warning passages.

You do not have to live in constant fear that you are losing God's love. His grip is stronger than yours.

A warning is simply that: a warning. It's not an indictment about what has already happened to you. A warning should lead to discernment about keeping a check on your life. Both Paul and the author of Hebrews are writing to believers about the apostasy of *other people* outside of their address. They are not giving current believers the label of apostate. They are speaking of people who were, at the time of their writing, *currently repudiating* Christ: rejecting Him, exulting in their sin, willfully turning away from Jesus, and deliberately ignoring correction from the church. They were not examining their hearts with humility. They were not asking God to show them their sin that they might repent and walk in holiness. Holiness was the furthest thing from their hearts. They were gleefully holding Jesus in contempt.

Ask yourself these questions:

Do you hate Jesus Christ?
Do you reject His sacrifice on the cross?

Do you deny that He is the Son of God?
Do you pretend like you don't know Him so you can run hard after idolatry and wickedness?

If those things are not true of you, then you can read the warning passages as *warnings*, not indictments about how God feels about you. Apostates don't fight for faith. Apostates don't examine the heart for sin. Apostates don't worry about God's love.

You do not have to live in constant fear that you are losing God's love. His grip is stronger than yours. The author of Hebrews doesn't lump in faithful believers with those who have left the faith. Rather, he points to those who have left the faith and draws a line in the sand. Don't live like them. Don't shrink back like them. Be steadfast in faith. *You are different!* "But we are not of those who shrink back and are destroyed," he writes, "but of those who have faith and preserve their souls" (Heb. 10:39).[7]

When you read the warning passages, it is fair and right to ask God to show you your sin, but it is also right to remind yourself that you are not one who shrinks back. You have faith. You live by faith, as have many, many saints throughout the church's history. That's why the author of Hebrews follows up his many warnings with the list of imperfect but faithful people who kept to the path of righteousness because they were kept by their faithful God.[8]

You can hold two truths in your heart at once: you struggle with sin *and* God still keeps you. The former does not cancel the latter. Live by faith, friend. Not by fear. Let God's perfect love drive out your fear (see 1 John 4:18).

---

7. On this subject, I am indebted to Collin Hansen for his helpful article "Warning Passages Ahead," The Gospel Coalition, January 9, 2012, https://www .thegospelcoalition.org/article/warning-passages-ahead/.
8. See Hebrews 11, which comes with great hope after the warning passages. There were many greatly flawed people in this list who finished in faithfulness. We should be encouraged by this list!

Read Psalm 139 in full again. Does this sound like a prayer from a man who lived in condemnation and fear? Or does this sound like a man who felt happily consumed and safely held by God's knowledge and love? The warning passages in Scripture are there for our benefit—so that we can learn from those who went before us and wandered away.[9] But those aren't the only passages in Scripture that speak to how we live as the people of God. Hold the tension of sober warning and faithful love. Know that God is more faithful than you and is perfectly capable of keeping you until the end. While our faithfulness is commanded, it is also upheld by our endlessly faithful God.

Read the warning passages and check your heart, but also read the passages below and check your heart, for though they may be harder to believe, they are equally true.

"Surely goodness and mercy shall follow me all the days of my life, and I shall dwell in the house of the LORD forever." (Ps. 23:6)

"The LORD redeems the life of his servants; none of those who take refuge in him will be condemned." (Ps. 34:22)

"Who is to condemn? Christ Jesus is the one who died— more than that, who was raised—who is at the right hand of God, who indeed is interceding for us." (Rom. 8:34)

"These things I have spoken to you, that my joy may be in you, and that your joy may be full." (John 15:11)

"For while we were still weak, at the right time Christ died for the ungodly." (Rom. 5:6)

9. 1 Corinthians 10:6, 11.

"Whoever confesses that Jesus is the Son of God, God abides in him, and he in God. So we have come to know and to believe the love that God has for us. God is love, and whoever abides in love abides in God, and God abides in him." (1 John 4:15–16)

Yes, you are weak, but oh, His love is strong. He Himself describes His love as steadfast and everlasting throughout Scripture. With that love He is able to keep you until the day you see Him face to face. Until then, His goodness and mercy are chasing you, keeping you on His path.

KNOWN AND KEPT

David's last plea is for God to lead him in the "the way everlasting" (Ps. 139:24). Note that David isn't taking full responsibility for his faithfulness. He is dependent on God to guide him in the way he should go. He knows that it is God who keeps him as he seeks to obey and stay on the Lord's path. What is the way everlasting? It is God's way. It is, as we've discussed in previous chapters, loving what God loves and hating what God hates. The way everlasting is paved with righteousness and mercy. It is traveled with obedience to His commands. It is believing in the good news of Christ crucified day after day after day. It is walking with Jesus and being molded into His image bit by bit, from one degree of glory to the next.

David helps us discern the way: "Let me hear in the morning of your steadfast love, for in you I trust. Make me know the way I should go, for to you I lift up my soul" (Ps. 143:8). Reminders of God's steadfast love will help us know how to live, which way to go, where the path of righteousness leads. As we sit on this side of the gospel story, we can be reminded of God's love every time we open our Bibles. Saturating our lives in Scripture will be absolutely necessary for discernment and growth. God uses His Word to sanctify us, to keep us on the path. He guides us in the way everlasting with Scripture.[10]

Even when our hearts have been cold, even when we've been led astray by sin, even when we were "brutish" toward Him in attitude, He is faithful to bring us back (Ps. 73:22). "Nevertheless, I am continually with you; you hold my right hand. You guide me with your counsel, and afterward you will receive me to glory" (Ps. 73:23–24). God guides, leads, and keeps us with His love. He is faithful to forgive us when we sin. You can trust Him to finish the work of salvation He began in you. You can believe that His attitude toward you is never brutish or cold.

Our Father isn't a grump with crossed arms and furrowed brows. He has open arms, running feet, and loving discipline. He will keep you on the path with His kind correction. So go ahead and ask Him to search your heart, to reveal any sin. Then repent. And believe that He loves you still. He is the God who keeps you.

○　○　○

for further thought:

1. Have you ever asked God to know your thoughts? If He already knows what you're thinking, why pray like David in verse 23?

2. What do you learn about God's character in Psalm 139:23–24?

---

10. One of the most helpful ways to saturate your life with God's Word is by memorizing it. See my book *Memorizing Scripture: The Basics, Blessings, and Benefits of Meditating on God's Word* for how and why to do it.

3. Have you ever prayed for God to show you your sin? If so, what has been the outcome of praying in this way?

4. Read Hebrews 12:3–11. How can God's discipline be a good thing for us? What might His discipline look like in our lives? What's the difference between discipline and punishment?

5. Have you lived with condemnation because of the warning passages in Scripture? How can we understand and revere those passages without living in condemnation? Discuss the difference between a warning and an indictment.

ROMANS 8:37

"No, in all these things we are more than conquerors through him who loved us."

9

Fully Known and Fully Loved

Will God Always Love Me?

I struggle to believe God's love doesn't hinge, at least in part, on my performance. I separate His love demonstrated in the gospel from His love for me personally, certain it must be based on merit. I know that's wrong, but pragmatically, I believe it.

I wrote those words many years ago, and when I read them while preparing to write this chapter, I felt sad for the insecure woman I used to be, the teenager who always felt guilty, the little girl who tried so hard to be good. I wanted to be completely loved for who I was, but the "who I was" part made that difficult. Sin always gets in the way of love in relationships.

Maybe that's you. Maybe that's why you picked up this book in the first place—to try to untangle your flaws from who you really are, hopeful that somehow that disassociation will make you lovable enough to deserve God's unmerited favor. But see, you knew what the problem was all along. It's not enough to be aware of our flaws. Sin has always been the real problem with us.

Maybe, like me, you have wanted God's love to be more than what you know about Jesus and the cross. Maybe you wanted Him to look at you with adoration because you're *you*, because you're just so lovely, so lovable, so interesting, so unique and talented and worthy of all His affection. Maybe you want to be loved not because God loved the world but because God loved *you*—just for being you.

That's often what we're after when we talk about God's love. We want to find a loophole in the doctrine of sin—our natural bent toward disobedience—and work out a way for us to be worthy of God's personal, invested love. You might even think, "I know God loves me because He sent Jesus, but I want Him to love me for *me*!" We want His love to be *more* than the gospel proof of it.

But God's love has substance. His love is not some gauzy, ethereal reaction to you being lovable. His love is tethered to real, hard proof of its existence. It originates in Him and is pinned securely to sacrifice and care, going beyond the brink to bring back an enemy, clean her up, and make her a daughter, a friend, a member of a kingdom of priests. What's more, we *need* His love to be attached to Jesus' work at the cross. This was our only hope of receiving His love and being eternally changed by it.

GOD'S LOVE HAS CONTENT

As we've discussed, we often imbue God's divine love with human traits and flaws. We also confuse the way He loves with the way we *want* to be loved. But God's love is indelibly inked with the blood of Jesus. We cannot disconnect His love from the cross. When we read that God so loved the world, the emphasis isn't so much on the generational and geographical reach as it is the *unloveliness* of the people He loves. Don Carson writes, "In John 3:16 God's love in sending the Lord Jesus is to be admired not because it is extended to so big a thing as the world, but to so bad a thing; not so many people, as to such wicked people."[1] If God's love was contingent upon our actions, skills, character qualities, and behavior, then His love would be as slippery and elusive as our worthiness of it. We could not keep His love because we could not continue being good enough to earn it. Carson says that God's love "emanates from his own character; it is not dependent on the loveliness of the loved, external to himself."[2] Because God *is* love, it is as though He says to us, "I love you anyway, not because you are attractive, but because it is my nature to love."[3] He loves because He purposed to love us. It was His plan to set His affections on us, not because we deserved it or would somehow earn it. His love comes from Himself, not from our worthiness. "He loves because love is one of his perfections, in perfect harmony with all his other perfections."[4]

Love that is earned by merit or attractiveness can be lost. How much better to be loved because it is God's nature to love us? How much better to be loved because God planned to save sinners through Jesus at the cross? How much better to be loved because the One who loves *is* love?

We cannot lose love like that. It goes far deeper than a sudden bloom of infatuation in response to a person's good features or traits. Those features or traits can be quickly lost when the ugliness of temper or selfishness or envy rise to the surface. Thankfully, God's love is more than that. He loved us in our ugliest, most

---

1. D. A. Carson, *The Difficult Doctrine of the Love of God* (Crossway, 1999), 17.
2. Ibid., 63.
3. Ibid., 63.
4. Ibid., 64.

unlovable state. Before we ever took a breath, He knew about all the things that make us unlovable, and He set His affections on us anyway. To be loved while you were the worst iteration of yourself is to reimagine the very idea of love itself.

Paul wrote that "God shows his love for us in that while we were still sinners, Christ died for us" (Rom. 5:8). You want to be sure that God knows you and loves you completely? You can't improve upon gospel love. This is the kind of love you're really after. God's love doesn't change in its existence or lavishness, but it does change *you*.

GOD'S LOVE TRANSFORMS

In human relationships, we laud the kind of love that lets another person be themselves. And to some extent, this is good and right. If my husband married me with the purpose of changing me, we would have had a problem from day one. But he doesn't have the kind of love that *can* change me. He loves me for the things that make me an attractive person to him, and his love makes me feel good and safe and valued. In his love, he pushes me to succeed and work hard in my field. He wants me to grow in Christ and fight sin, as I want for him. But his love has limits. His love cannot *make* my heart different. His love cannot change the essence of my being.

Nor can mine for him.

God's love, however, changes us at our very core. When He saves us through faith in Jesus, God gives us new hearts, new identities, new desires. We were dead; He made us alive.[5] We were enemies; He made us friends.[6] We were moved from the

5. Ephesians 2:4–5.
6. Romans 5:10; John 15:14.

kingdom of darkness to the kingdom of Jesus.[7] We have been transformed! And in His love, He continues to transform us, as we discussed in chapter 8. He refuses to leave us to our devices but sanctifies us instead—making us more and more like His Son.[8] His love changes our desires, renews our minds, and sets our hearts on what is above.[9]

This is the kind of love we are desperate for. Though we might desire love that cushions and comforts, what we get is love that transforms. Love that does not let us go. Love that refuses to let us run after sin and so runs after us with correction. And that is ultimate comfort and assurance! God's love at the cross makes us worthy of it! Remember imputed righteousness? Jesus became your sin so you could become the righteousness of God. No matter who you were or how you lived before you knew Jesus, God's love obliterates every shard of brokenness. He makes you brand new. "Never, never underestimate the power of the love of God to break down and transform the most amazingly hard individuals."[10] That's what God's perfect love has done for us in Christ.

Confident of this love, how then should we live?

LIVING KNOWN, LIVING LOVED

Psalm 139 celebrates all the ways God intimately knows us, stays near us, is invested in our lives, and suffuses our lives with meaning. After grappling with His omniscience and steadfast love, we must respond with faith. We must believe that we are known and loved, and we must live like we're known and loved. Like my journal entry at the beginning of this chapter, we might

---

7. Colossians 1:13.
8. 2 Corinthians 3:18; 4:16.
9. See Colossians 2–3.
10. D. A. Carson, *The Difficult Doctrine of the Love of God*, 81.

acknowledge these truths about God's attitude toward us mentally while still practically living as though His love can be won and lost every day. But much of the Christian life is lived by faith, so we must return to proof of God's love over and over by saturating our minds with His Word. Scripture tells us what's true when our hearts feel differently.

So let's look at a passage of Scripture that helps us live known and loved in light of God's gospel expression of care at the cross. Paul writes in Romans:

> What then shall we say to these things? If God is for us, who can be against us? He who did not spare his own Son but gave him up for us all, how will he not also with him graciously give us all things? Who shall bring any charge against God's elect? It is God who justifies. Who is to condemn? Christ Jesus is the one who died—more than that who was raised— who is at the right hand of God, who indeed is interceding for us. Who shall separate us from the love of Christ? Shall tribulation, or distress, or persecution, or famine, or nakedness, or danger, or sword? As it is written, "For your sake we are being killed all the day long; we are regarded as sheep to be slaughtered." No, in all these things we are more than conquerors through him who loved us. For I am sure that neither death nor life, nor angels nor rulers, nor things present nor things to come, nor powers, nor height nor depth, nor anything else in all creation, will be able to separate us from the love of God in Christ Jesus our Lord. (Rom. 8:31–39)

You might notice a familiar kind of symmetry in those final verses. Where Psalm 139 praises the expansiveness of God's knowledge, presence, and love, Romans 8 also extols the geographical and transcendent reach of God's love for us in Jesus. There is literally nothing in space or time that can separate us from His love. Not internal condemnation, not the worst imagined suffering, not rulers that come to power in this world, not our greatest earthly fears. *Nothing* can separate you from God's love.

But this close, squeezed-in love is wound up tightly in the death of Jesus. So we must preach the gospel to ourselves over and over again to keep that love front and center. When we forget Jesus, we forget who we are. When we forget His sacrifice or grow cold to it, we forget that we are loved. We forget we are His.

Paul's praise for the certainty of God's love in Christ helps us live known and loved. He reminds us not to forget God's love, not to fear its loss, and to let it motivate us to walk in obedience to Him.

Don't Forget God's Love

The Bible is filled with declarations of God's care for us, no doubt because we so easily forget the nature and shape and impermeability of His love. Romans 8 reminds us that God doesn't mildly or generically love us. Rather, He is *for* us. "If God is for us, who can be against us?" Paul asks (Rom. 8:31). God's heart is inclined toward us, not away. For, not against.

God doesn't "fall in love" like we do. He doesn't grow enamored with us over time. No, He set His affections upon us before the world existed.

This truth encourages us in two ways. First, no foe is stronger than He is. There is no adversary or opposition to God's purposes that will win in the end. He wins, and because of Christ, we are eternally safe in His victory. Second, God desires our good.

Though He allows suffering and trials that can refine our faith and fuel our dependency on Him, He does so for our best interests. We often read Romans 8:28 in isolation, but when coupled with verse 29, its meaning is amplified. "And we know that for those who love God all things work together for good, for those who are called according to his purpose. For those whom he foreknew (or, *foreloved*) he also predestined to be conformed to the image of his Son, in order that he might be the firstborn among many brothers" (Rom. 8:28–29).

God works things together for good for those who belong to Him, and the reason we can be sure of this is because He has always planned to sanctify those whom He set His affections on. Remember, God doesn't "fall in love" like we do. He doesn't grow enamored with us over time. No, He set His affections upon us before the world existed.[11] His love is purposeful. Committed. Faithful. It emanates from His perfect being, not grown from our mercurial goodness.

How can we remember and feel confident in this kind of love and care? Look at Romans 8:32. God didn't spare His own Son to extend saving grace, love, and mercy to us. If He didn't spare Jesus' life to save us, why would He hold back what we need to live in His love? He has given us what we need to endure in this life, and He's promised to give His kingdom in the next.[12] "In giving his Son he gave everything. The cross is the guarantee of the continuing, unfailing generosity of God."[13]

Do not forget that God loves you. Every morning when you wake up, remember the gospel. Remember that God sent Jesus to rescue you and make you His own. He didn't do it because

11. D. A. Carson, *The Difficult Doctrine of the Love of God*, 61.
12. Romans 8:17.
13. John Stott, *The Message of Romans* (InterVarsity Press, 1994), 255.

you were lovely or enchanting—but rather because you *weren't*. Because you couldn't be. I couldn't be. This is real, perfect love. When you feel like His love is dissipating in a fog of doubt, turn to His Word. Let the truth chase your doubts away like the warmth of the rising sun burns off the early morning mist.

Don't Fear the Loss of God's Love

Romans 8 also helps us walk through the Christian life with certainty that we cannot lose God's love. While we discussed feeling fearful of the warning passages in Scripture in the last chapter, Paul encourages us to enjoy the immutable love of God. In Christ, you cannot be condemned by your sin or the enemy. In Christ you are firmly enclosed in His love. In Romans 8:34, Paul tells us that Jesus' death and resurrection ensures our right standing before God. There's no more condemnation because Christ's payment secured our righteousness. Nothing that happens to you in this life can cancel out His atonement. Your heart is safe in His love. No source of physical or spiritual suffering can sever you from the love that hems you in. Not even death itself.

Look at the list of potential threats to God's love for us in verses 34–49:

Charge of guilt	*Death*
Condemnation	*Life*
Tribulation	*Present*
Distress	*Future*
Persecution	*Powers*
Famine	*Height*
Nakedness	*Depth*
Danger	*Anything else in creation*
Sword	

Now, remember the encouragements about God's closeness and care in Psalm 139:

> *You know when I sit down and when I rise.*
> *You know my thoughts, my words, my steps.*
> *You hem me in, You lay Your hand upon me.*
> *You are in heaven, Sheol, the early morning, the depths of*
> *the sea, the dark, the light.*
> *You saw me in my mother's womb, You see my sins, my heart,*
> *my thoughts.*

God is always near and ever close. And nothing can get between you and His love for you. Nothing. So in a sense, you can say to the wickedness and trials of the world, "Do your best! I am safe in Christ!" Even if you lose your life, you cannot lose His love. And in death you are with Christ, so there's not even a true loss there—only gain!

As Paul says, "We are more than conquerors through him who loved us" (Rom. 8:37). God's love secured our victory over sin and death at the cross. It is anchored in a purposeful collision of sacrifice and justice and mercy and grace. You do not have to fear losing His love. It is yours, ever yours. Live in it!

Respond to God's Love with Obedience

When I was in high school, my mom would aways stop me as I headed out the door, car keys in my hand. "Remember who you are and whose you are!" she'd say. In other words, remember who you belong to and live accordingly. While she was referring to our family and its values, ultimately, she was reminding me that I belonged to Jesus and that how I lived each day should reflect that. "Make choices in alignment with your identity."

Hopefully by this point in this book, you know you're known and you know you're loved. Now it's time to respond to God's intimate care in a way that aligns with our identity in Christ. Jesus makes it clear in John 15 that we respond to God's love with obedience. "If you keep my commandments, you will abide in my love, just as I have kept my Father's commandments and abide in His love" (v. 10). Jesus is showing us that as He obeyed His Father as a response to the Father's love, we too obey Him as a response to His love. He has shown us what obedience looks like, not only because He is holy but because obedience is the right response to love.

Don't mix up the order, though! We don't obey to *be* loved. We obey because we *are* loved. Obedience is how we abide in His love. Jude said it this way: "Keep yourselves in the love of God" (Jude 21). There are two things going on here. First, we live in God's love by obeying Him. Second, we obey Him because He enables us to with the help of His Spirit. We abide, and He keeps. It's a both/and situation.

In Galatians, Paul addresses obedience, connecting it to being known by God.

> Formerly, when you did not know God, you were enslaved to those that by nature are not gods. But now that you have come to know God, or rather *to be known by God*, how can you turn back again to the weak and worthless elementary principles of the world, whose slaves you want to become once more? (Gal. 4:8–9)

There's a demarcation here that's important to note. Being known by God means living for Him rather than for yourself. Why would you want to return to the things that never satisfy and only lead you to sin when you have been *known* by God. Paul is reminding the Galatians of who and whose they are. You're known by God. You're loved by God. Now embrace that identity by walking in obedience to God.

We often confuse joy with being deliriously happy, but true biblical joy is evidenced by peace and confidence that God will make all things right in the end.

Obedience isn't a drudgery response to God's love, though it may seem that way at first glance. Obedience is also a source of joy. God knows that these known and loved hearts of ours will be miserable in sin but joyful in obedience. He knows what will bring us satisfaction and what will leave us hungry and weak. When we obey His commands and live closely to His Word, we will be filled with the joy of Christ. Jesus said, "These things I have spoken to you, that my joy may be in you, and that your joy may be full" (John 15:11). We have access to the joy of Jesus! As we obey God, confident of our right standing before Him, we ought to be the most joyful people on the earth.

We often confuse joy with being deliriously happy, but I think joy is weightier than that. It's thicker, deeper, stouter, and more complex. True biblical joy is evidenced by peace and confidence that God will make all things right in the end. It's a surety in your soul that He will right the wrongs and end our suffering and come out the Victor over the enemy. We know how this story ends. We know Christ will return, that He will vanquish His foes, that we will be with Him forever. That should give us deep and abiding confidence in a world of uncertainty, suffering, and looming persecution. We don't have to lose our minds in fear. We don't have to be anxious that God has forgotten us. Rather, we obey Him with deep-seated joy that cannot be stolen from us, for God's love is the fixed point in our lives. Nothing separates us from it.

Knowing who we are and whose we are should lead to evangelism. It should cultivate love for our enemies in hopes that they might become our siblings in Christ. Living loved should invigorate our efforts to get the good news of soul-transforming gospel love to those who are living in darkness. "We owe others the gospel."[14]

KNOWN AND LOVED

No singular book can contain all there is to say about the omniscience and love of God. I could point you to many more and better written books on these subjects, and we would still have only scratched the surface.[15] But Psalm 139 has given us much to chew on as we examine God's knowledge and love for us. I hope that as you work to understand who He is and how He describes His character, you'll untangle your feelings of contempt from God's perfect love.

He has never left you and never will. He has delighted in you, and He has disciplined you, and He has loved you with an everlasting love.

That's kind of the whole point, actually.

You were contemptible. So was I.

But God condescended to know us and love us anyway. He has removed our guilt and our shame and has made us holy instead. He has pressed in close, squeezing in tight around us with safety and

14. D. A. Carson, *The Difficult Doctrine of the Love of God*, 83.
15. Please see the list of recommended resources for books that will help round out your theology of God's omniscience and love.

care. He has knitted our earthly forms together with purpose and creativity. He has kept track of every thought and care, has ordained every day and every step. He has given you a new identity as His child and kept watch over you while you slept. He has canceled the record of debt that stood against you and clothed you in His best robe of righteousness. He has saved you. And He will sanctify you until the day you see Him face to face. He has never left you and never will. He has delighted in you, and He has disciplined you, and He has loved you with an everlasting love. He has called you daughter or son, and He has shared with you all that He has to be enjoyed with Him forever.

Does this sound like a God who doesn't like you?

As you close this book, my prayer is that you will douse your doubts with the truth of Scripture every time they creep in to make you feel beyond God's love. We fight lies with truth, and God's Word is truth. I pray that you, "being rooted and grounded in love, may have strength to comprehend with all the saints what is the breadth and length and height and depth, and to know the love of Christ that surpasses knowledge, that you may be filled with all the fullness of God" (Eph. 3:17–19).

God's love is immeasurable and beyond our understanding. But He knows. Yes, He *knows*. And He loves. Oh, how He loves.

○ ○ ○

for further thought:

1. Why is it better to be loved while we were still an enemy of God than to be loved for lovable qualities? How is it good news for us that God's love is connected to Jesus' death and resurrection?

2. Look at Psalm 139 and Romans 8:31–39. Write out the similarities you see in these passages pertaining to God's knowledge and love. What have you learned about God's love that you didn't understand or recognize before?

3. What in your life makes you fear the loss of God's love for you personally? How does Romans 8:31–39 challenge your fear?

4. Read John 15:1–17. Why is obedience the right response of love? How did Jesus model this to us?

5. How does living known and loved by God change the way you will live from now on? What have you learned about God's character in Psalm 139 that encourages and challenges you most?

Acknowledgments

Of the books I've written thus far, this one has been most difficult to pen. Attempting to capture the divine attributes of God's love and omniscience has kept me awake at night, worrying I wouldn't get it *right*. After all, how can you accurately focus on two of God's traits without diminishing the rest of them? But I realized in my research, reading, thinking, and writing that God's Word will do the work of teaching us what we need to know about Him. Psalm 139 helps us develop a right understanding of His character, and if you glean nothing more from this book than a more expansive view of His love for you from David's prayer, then I can ask for nothing more or better.

I am grateful for my editor, Catherine Parks, who enthusiastically represented me and this book idea to Moody Publishers. Both she and the team at Moody have cheered me on, prayed for me, and supported *Known and Loved* in word and deed. Being so cared for by a publishing team is a true gift to any author. Many thanks to Kaylee Dunn for listening to my abstract and obtuse ideas for cover art and developing something that captured both the theme of the book and the warmth of "rising on the wings of the dawn." Pam Pugh, you are so good at what you do. Your edits make my work stronger, and you've taught me how to write more clearly. If I never learn the difference between toward and towards, it won't be your fault.

While I never got to meet Pastor Tim Keller, his ministry has had a profound impact on my understanding of the gospel and of God's love. As you will see reflected in many of the footnotes, his work has shaped my theology and given me much wisdom to draw from. I am not sure I could have written this book without his own books and sermons that taught me much about God. I am grateful for saints like him who left much work behind and disciple us from heaven.

To the folks in my Sunday school class at church, thank you for patiently putting up with me every time I pushed God's love and knowledge into our discussions. If I'm working on a book, the themes inevitably come out in Sunday school. I'm sorry for how annoying that must be, but I'm grateful for a safe place to work out my questions. The people of Grace Bible Fellowship are at the heart of my reason for writing this book. Thank you for praying for me while I wrote it. I love you so very, very much. But wow, does God love you more!

I will always dig deeper into Scripture when I know I've got a group of women showing up at my house on Tuesdays at noon for Bible study. Lisa, Kay, Linda, Kathy, Joan, and Genesis: you bless me more than you know. Your desire to know God in His Word is something to behold. Thank you for praying for me while I wrote this book.

I'm grateful for Janie Williams and Leah Finn for cheering me on in weekly (daily?) Marco Polo videos. Your friendship means the world to me, and the Sourdough Squad will never break up. My mother and sister kept me going while I wrote. They offered many, many distractions through our never-ending, unfailing, steadfast text thread. To count my mom and sister as my closest friends is too sweet for words.

As I worked on this book, I had countless conversations with my husband on our early morning walks while I tried to organize my thoughts on Psalm 139. There is a certain advantage to being married to your pastor, and I am deeply grateful to have a husband who loves God's Word and patiently answers all my questions. I picked his brain clean. William, I love you. As this idea grew into an actual book, the love of God became a comforting heartbeat in your sermons that I looked for each week. Thank you for growing with me in the same direction. And you were right. I did finish the book on time.

To Isaiah and Ian, who always have to deal with a writing mom who has summer deadlines, thank you for giving me quiet mornings to write when school was out. I love you as much as any mother could, but I hope you know God loves you more. He made you with love and care and purpose, and somehow, He saw fit to put you in my arms. You radiate His glory, and you fill my life with joy.

Lord, I am sorry I have so long doubted and questioned Your love for me. It bursts from the pages of Your Word with brilliance and glory and certainty. Love is sacrifice. I see it now.

Recommended Resources

Below are the books that were helpful to me as I worked through the doctrine of God's love, Psalm 139, Romans 8, and other concepts in this book. I commend each of them to you for further reading.

Because He Loves Me: How Christ Transforms Our Daily Life by Elyse M. Fitzpatrick, Crossway, 2008.

The Difficult Doctrine of the Love of God by D. A. Carson, Crossway, 1999.

Heaven by Randy Alcorn, Tyndale, 2004.

The Message of Romans by John Stott, InterVarsity Press, 1994.

The Message of John by Bruce Milne, InterVarsity Press, 1993.

The Pleasures of God: Meditations on God's Delight in Being God by John Piper, Multnomah Books, 2000.

Prayer: Experiencing Awe and Intimacy with God by Timothy Keller, Penguin Books, 2014.

Rediscovering Jonah: The Secret of God's Mercy by Timothy Keller, Penguin Books, 2018.

Walking with God through Pain and Suffering by Timothy Keller, Penguin Books, 2013.

What God Has to Say About Our Bodies: How the Gospel Is Good News for Our Physical Selves by Sam Allberry, Crossway, 2021.

GLENNAMARSHALL.COM/NEWSLETTER

Reclaiming the art of Scripture memorization

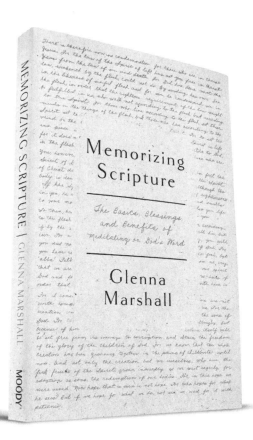